Becoming Verbal with

Childhood
Apraxia

MSL
Marshalla Speech and Language

Originally published as *How to Help Children with Speech Imitation*, © 1997

© 2001 by Pamela Marshalla. All rights reserved
Printed in Canada

Marshalla Speech and Language
11417 - 124th Avenue Northeast
Kirkland, WA 98033
www.pammarshalla.com

All citations from Jean Piaget were taken from *Piaget's Theory of Intellectual Development*, Herbert Ginsburg and Sylvia Opper, Prentice-Hall, Inc., Englewood Cliffs, NJ, 1969.

ISBN 0-9707060-6-5

Dedication

This book is dedicated to three fabulous women from the University of Illinois who permitted me to be an original thinker.

- To Dr. Joan Good Erickson, who taught me to be thorough in observation and assessment, and always to carry a broken toy in my diagnostic box.
- To Dr. Lillian Katz, who showed me how to see the world through the eyes of a preschool child.
- To Dr. Merle B. Karnes, who permitted me to be a teacher and a writer at an early age.

Contents

Introduction   7

1: The Integral Relationship of Childhood Apraxia and Imitation   9

2: The Entertaining Variety of Sound   13

3: The Power of Crowd Noise   21

4: Creating One Voice for Imitation Development   29

5: Laughter Encourages Turn Taking   37

6: Learning to Take Turns in Dialogue   45

7: Mutual Imitation: The Most Important Stage   63

8: Imitating the Repertoire: A Significant Breakthrough for Imitation Skill   71

9: New Sounds and Words: Reaching Success in the Final Stage   83

Glossary   107

Introduction
The Heart of the Problem

Let's face it: Apraxic children can be a puzzle. Although they can be bright, apraxic children don't start talking until two or three years of age or older. Each word they learn comes slowly and with tremendous difficulty. Articulation is always quite poor. Because it is difficult for them to say words and pronounce phonemes, apraxic children can remain minimally verbal and highly unintelligible for a long time. Those of us who live and work with apraxic children have to try awfully hard to get them to speak well.

Most speech and language pathologists approach the apraxic child with the assumption that he is able to imitate. We assume that if we present a specific sound or word often enough, the non-verbal apraxic child will eventually catch on and repeat it after us. But time after time we find we are met with a silent stare, a topic switch, a refusal, or a poor response that leaves us wondering whether the child actually heard us.

Based on the observations of Jean Piaget and his pioneering research into the development of imitation in young children, *Becoming Verbal with Childhood Apraxia* exposes the truth that apraxic children cannot imitate. It presents a methodology designed to facilitate verbal output in young children with severe apraxia of speech. These techniques have helped children begin to talk and use a wide variety of words and phrases.

We teach children *how* to assimilate new sounds and words by structuring individual therapy sessions around dialogue. Through this method, children become more active in their own therapy and discover how to:

- Talk more
- Pay attention to their own utterances
- Attend the speech of others
- Rehearse their sounds and words
- Master their own productions
- Say new sounds and words at will

Not all apraxic children will make it through the entire process. Some will fail to learn how to spontaneously imitate new sounds or words during the course of their childhood; others will not learn it at any time in their lives. Most apraxic children, however, can learn to imitate speech and language skills, and they become quite proficient at it.

If you are the parent of an apraxic child, I hope that the ideas presented here will help you understand your child's needs. If you are a therapist, especially a speech and language pathologist, it is my hope that these approaches rooted in the intelligence of Jean Piaget will revolutionize your therapy as much as it did mine.

PLEASE NOTE: The most current label for this disorder is *childhood apraxia*. This term has been used in addition to older terms. Also, male gender pronouns (i.e., *he, him, his*) are used throughout to refer to the client with childhood apraxia.

Chapter One

The Integral Relationship of
Childhood Apraxia and
Imitation

Imitation is a basic human ability, an essential element in general child development, and a critical component for learning to speak. Imitation is the ability to follow an action or manner, to copy, to duplicate, to mimic, to reproduce, or to assume the appearance of a variety of movements, including speech movements. Humans have the ability to imitate facial expressions, sounds, words, intonation patterns, accents, gestures, actions, and emotions. Early in life, we can repeat what others say with great precision, amazing accuracy, and simple ease. It takes most babies less than one year to learn the mature imitation skills necessary to say words like *momma*, *daddy*, or *bye-bye*. Most children learn to imitate the majority of sounds in our language, including thousands of words, before they enter elementary school.

Do you have a typical child who began to talk when he was about one year of age? What words did he say? How did he begin to say the words? A child's first words may include any number of possibilities:

Mamma	night	computer	shoe	meow
Dada	down	go	doggie	more
bye-bye	bottle	car	elephant	yea
hi	juice	eat	TV	no

If you have observed the emergence of first words in an average one-year-old child, you have witnessed the birth of mature imitation. What an achievement! The appearance of a child's first words is usually an exciting event that is met with great joy in the family. What did you do when you heard your child's first word? Perhaps you clapped, smiled, repeated the word excitedly, praised him, or looked for the first situation in which you could show off his skill to others.

Until he is able to read, all words that a youngster speaks are imitations of words he has heard from parents, siblings, friends, relatives, and neighbors, as well as those spoken in movies, television programs, commercials, musical recordings, and by talking toys and computers. That is a lot of words! The vocabulary expressed by the typical five-year-old numbers in the tens of thousands, and the ideas he can express with these words are quite complicated. Kindergarten children can be long-winded as they relate adorable stories and amusing events with words that they learned through speech imitation. By five years of age, most children can pronounce all the phonemes of their native language with great accuracy. All young children make a few simple errors, but overall the five-year-old is highly intelligible. We can understand him virtually all the time.

When we think of the word *imitation*, most of us think of mature imitation, such as when a one-year-old child can hear a modeled sound or word and repeat it. But children are not born with fully mature imitation skill. The skill begins primitively and evolves during the course of the child's first year of life. How does the ability to imitate begin, and how does it come to maturity? That information is what can help the young apraxic child learn to speak well.

The House of Imitation

In Jean Piaget's writings on childhood intellectual development, he described four basic stages in the development of imitation in infancy, beginning with primitive skills just after birth and mature skills at about one year of age. These stages might be equated to the steps one takes when constructing a house: from foundation and frame, to walls and roof.

Likewise, imitation is a linear construction of skills assembled in a certain order. These steps are called the Stages of Imitation.

Each stage includes certain skills. By the first birthday, the average child possesses all the skills necessary to engage in the most mature level of imitation and begins to say a small number of intelligible words. The child's "house of imitation" will have been built, and from that point forward he will not have to learn about the process any more. Instead, he will use that process to acquire a fully functional expressive speech and language system. We shall use Piaget's stages as the framework for the ideas in this book.

Childhood Apraxia and Imitation

Every speech and language pathologist knows that children with apraxia have great difficulty learning to imitate speech sounds and words like other children. Many apraxic children are almost silent as babies and toddlers, and they do not speak much at all until three, four, or five years of age—or even older. A serious delay in expressive speech can be frustrating or frightening for the parents. They might begin to ask, "Will he ever talk?" The joy they assumed would come with his first words becomes long overdue. Then, when the child finally does begin to talk, his utterances can be fleeting and difficult to understand.

The stages of imitation development that are observed in typical children can be relied upon to understand the difficulty with which apraxic children acquire speech. Still, there are differences. Whereas typical babies develop through these stages quickly and easily and complete the process by age one, children with apraxia have much more trouble, including:

- LATE EMERGENCE: Many apraxic children do not begin the process of imitation development on time.
- SLOW MATURATION: Most apraxic children take longer to advance from one stage of imitation to the next.
- STAGNATION: Most apraxic children get stuck at early stages and do not progress on to advanced stages
- INABILITY: Some severely apraxic children never do begin the imitation process at all
- SCATTER: Periodically, an apraxic child will advance too quickly to the higher stages of imitation, skipping the earlier stages or leaving them incomplete

Good builders know that each stage of building construction must be completed well or problems will appear later on. For example, a frame built on a shaky foundation will not stand, and a roof built on an insecure frame will not hold up. Although apraxic children can have problems in many areas of expressive speech and language development—including oral-motor skills, vocal development, and more—they do not have the ability to acquire mature speech-imitation skills. Thus, they cannot build their house of imitation in order to develop a fully functional expressive speech system.

Our Goal

The goal is to discover how to help young apraxic children become more vocal and to imitate speech. The following chapters will describe the essential elements of learning to imitate speech as it relates to "average" children up to one year of age. The problems apraxic children have at each stage will be discussed, including guidelines, techniques, and activities that are designed to help them acquire these skills. With an improved ability to imitate sounds and words, most, but not all, young children with severe childhood apraxia can begin to talk and become more intelligible.

Chapter Two

The Entertaining Variety of Sound

Babies spend an enormous amount of time rehearsing sounds before their words emerge. We call them *pre-speech vocalizations*. Pre-speech vocalizations are those spontaneous and self-generated sounds that are made without correspondence to a specific idea or meaning. For example, a grunt is a pre-speech vocalization. A grunt may be produced when the child is hard at work, like when he's filling his diaper, but it does not mean diaper, hard work, or, "Someone come and change my diaper." It is simply a spontaneous sound that accompanies a specific bodily function. Adults then interpret by adding meaning. For example, in response to a baby's grunt one might say, "Oh-oh. I think you need a new diaper."

Babies produce many such sounds spontaneously during this period including coos, goos, laughs, nasal sounds, grunts, growls, squeals, shouts, gurgles, raspberries, whispers, and several vowels (V). About six months of age, babies learn to say a few consonants (C) and a few simple consonant and vowel (CV) combinations. Between six and twelve months of age, babies learn to combine their consonants and vowels into increasingly complex sequences with the process known as *babbling*. Babies who are vocal enjoy making these pre-speech vocalizations, and they spend a significant amount of time rehearsing and experimenting with them by practicing them with a wide variety of pitch, intensity, intonation, resonance, tension, length, and loudness patterns. *Vocal play*, the rich rehearsal and experimentation with a wide variety of sounds, helps them to learn the most primitive aspects of speech-imitation skill.

Have you ever observed babies making sounds by themselves? Babies typically repeat target sounds as a form of play and self-entertainment, embellishing each trial with increasing focus. In so doing, a baby begins to recognize his own voice through its tactile, proprioceptive, and auditory properties. He begins to experiment with these properties and to make specific sounds at will, recognizing the similarities and differences of sound sensation as he produces them.

Pre-speech vocal play is a child's self-expression and solo experimentation. It's the means by which the child puts together the ingredients he needs to make the foundation for the house of speech imitation. He experiments with his own voice and with a wide variety of speech features. In so doing, he discovers his capacity for speech production in the same way he discovers other movements: through play and systematic experimentation.

At this foundational level, it is the child's ability to engage in purposeful and repetitive sound play that begins the process of imitation development. Piaget called this process that teaches the child to perceive and repeat his own actions *circular reactions*. In a circular reaction, a baby does the same pattern over and over again until it becomes a learned habit that can be incorporated into other actions. In speech development, this is evidenced by the baby's ability to produce specific sounds spontaneously and consistently at will.

Children with Childhood Apraxia

How does pre-speech vocal play relate to the imitative abilities of children with apraxia? As was stated earlier, the apraxic baby or toddler tends to be quiet. As a result, most apraxic children:

- Spend little time rehearsing pre-speech vocalizations
- Spend little time discovering how to make sound consistently
- Spend little time listening to and developing good auditory discrimination of their own voice

- Spend little time "feeling" pre-speech vocalizations and developing the tactile and proprioceptive discrimination skills of sound-making
- Are slow in learning how to produce their own spontaneous sounds at will

Rehearsal of pre-speech vocalizations and the development of early imitation skills go hand-in-hand at this most primitive stage of imitation learning. Each affects the other in a reciprocal arrangement. Think of it this way: The fun of producing sound begets the rehearsal of more sound, which facilitates better attention to sound, which allows the child to discover similarities and differences between sounds, which encourages him to produce particular sounds consistently over time. The apraxic child lacks in those skills. He does not make much sound, therefore he does not learn to attend to sound well, discriminate sound well, or develop an ability to produce sounds consistently under his own volition.

Using Sound to Build Early Imitative Ability

The first task in the development of speech-imitation skill in apraxic children is to encourage the production of a wide variety of spontaneous speech sounds through the experience of vocal play. It is not specific consonants, vowels, or words that are the issue; those will arise later. The key sounds are those that babies produce before six months of age, or before babbling emerges. The goal is to help apraxic children learn to produce more pre-speech vocalizations, to experiment with them, and to begin to recognize the similarities and differences between them in a playful milieu.

The specific vocalizations the child produces aren't important. The primary concern is with his ability to make all kinds of sounds, to attend to them, to play with them by altering their features, and eventually to become consistent in their production. In essence, what is encouraged is the child's ability to produce sound, not his ability to imitate us. This helps him begin to regulate and control his own speech behavior.

Listen to Your Child

At this level of imitation development, it is important to discover what makes the apraxic child more vocal. Is it a car ride? Is it while playing in the sand? Is it during fingerpainting? Is it while swinging and singing? Is it while chasing a huge ball around the back yard? Is it during bath time?

The notion of functional communication has dominated the field of speech and language therapy for more than twenty years. During those two decades the important process of rehearsing sound has been diminished. Much of our therapy today for young apraxic children is designed to stimulate verbal expression by focusing on the use of functional words and phrases in everyday communication routines. For example, we teach minimally verbal apraxic children to say "juice" when they want juice, and to say "bye-bye" when it's time to go.

But, a child's earliest form of sound production and imitation arises spontaneously as he engages in self-expressive vocal play for entertainment and experimentation. His intelligence is dominated by sensorimotor experiences that are reinforced as fun ways to discover the tactile, proprioceptive, and auditory sensations of sound productions. Little babies do make sound to satisfy pragmatic functions like showing, obtaining, refusing, or asking. But they make more sound purely for the sake of enjoyment.

There are many ways to provide vocal play experiences for the apraxic child. The following is a list of ideas.

Copy for Parents

Bath time

Bath time is one of the best times to work on pre-speech sound awareness and production. The child is in a small, acoustically reverberating little box of a room. He is being bathed in warm water and is surrounded by fun items like soap, bubbles, washcloths, pouring containers, and toys. During a bath, parents can shift their focus from "getting the child clean" to "having fun and vocalizing together while getting clean." The idea is to create an open forum for free expression of sound and then to play with these sounds.

Bedtime and Wake Up

Bedtime is another wonderful opportunity to facilitate free and spontaneous sound play. Apraxic children who talk to themselves, whether using sounds or words, can be left alone to jabber away contentedly until they fall asleep or after they wake up. This is a perfect opportunity for pre-speech vocal play. This rich sound play activity, called *crib speech*, does not need to be curtailed. You might even consider fastening an unbreakable infant mirror in the crib or on the wall next to your child's bed so he can watch himself make sounds.

Singing

Singing is a great way to model continuous speech behavior for sound discovery, experimentation, and entertainment. Sing any-thing—kids songs, oldies, commercials, or hymns. Dig through your memory for those songs you loved as a kid:

- "The Itsy-Bitsy Spider"
- "Old McDonald Had a Farm"
- "Mary Had a Little Lamb"
- "The ABC Song"
- "London Bridges"
- "This Little Light of Mine"

Sing along with the radio, sing together as a family, and sing alone to your child. Dance and sing, hop and sing, and cuddle and sing. Do finger puppets or games and sing. Don't worry about your child learning the words to the songs. Teach him to make sound and sing for fun.

Tickling and Roughhousing

Tickling and roughhousing are easy ways to encourage sound production and sound play in the apraxic child. This type of play typically facilitates a lot of sound output. During roughhouse play children usually laugh, squeal, scream, shout, giggle, pant, growl, whoop, and holler. Get the whole family involved so that everyone is making noise. This will encourage your apraxic child to make sound during the fun and afterward as he remembers the event and tries to initiate the play again.

Boxes, Forts, and Houses

Do you remember how much you loved to play inside large boxes or under blankets as a child? Part of the fun has to do with privacy and imagination, and part of it has to do with the dramatic acoustic changes that occur in an enclosed space. Sound coming from outside the box is muffled and quiet, but inside the box even the most quiet and insignificant sound made by the child become salient and important. Children love to whisper in a large box because they can hear themselves so well. It is a great place to encourage pre-speech vocalizations in apraxic children.

Tubes, Hoses, Funnels, and Rolls

Children love to make sounds in these toys, and they are excellent for facilitating sound play with an apraxic child. Provide your child with empty paper-towel rolls, toilet-paper rolls, wrapping-paper rolls, rubber and vinyl tubes (aquarium tubing works great), kitchen funnels, new oil-changing funnels, huge empty carpet rolls, or a piece of hose. Teach the child to use them to make sound, especially vowel sounds. Teach him to play "telephone" by talking through tubes and rolls.

Blow Toys

Teach the apraxic child to blow through horns, whistles, harmonicas, and other blow toys, and to blow bubbles. Blowing is not speech, per say, and the purpose of these activities is not to teach the child to blow through the item. The purpose of blow toys is to teach the child to inhale and exhale with increasingly greater awareness and control so that he can do so during the production of speech sounds later. Teach him to inhale deeply and to blow long and short. Also, blow cotton balls, tissue balls, table tennis balls, and mommy's hair. Blow out candles at home with adult supervision.

Kazoos

The kazoo is probably one of the greatest tools we have for encouraging vocalizations in apraxic children. Unlike a blowing toy, a kazoo forces a child to use his voice to make it work. For emphasis, play with kazoos in the large boxes or homemade houses and forts. Use kazoos to "sing" the happy birthday song, holiday songs, and general children's songs before your child has enough words to sing them. Make loud and soft sounds in the kazoo, long and short sounds, and high and low pitches. Pretend to be a band by marching around the room while sounding your kazoos. A young, severely apraxic child who has few sounds and words at his disposal often finds great joy in using a kazoo for self-expression.

First Games Sounds

Most children enjoy saying the simple sounds associated with early games. Say, "Boo!" while playing Peek-a-Boo, or, "Wee-wee-wee" while playing This Little Piggy Went to Market. Again, the apraxic child often learns general sounds more easily. Once he can say them, provide multiple opportunities throughout the week to practice.

Animal, Monster, and Vehicle Sounds

Well before they say words, most children learn to say animal, monster, and vehicle sounds, like the *meow* of a cat, the *growl* of a monster, or the *vroom* of a car. These sounds can be easier for an apraxic child to say, so they also can be easier to stimulate. For young, severely apraxic children who have little means of vocal or verbal communication, motor, crashing, screeching, monster, and animal sounds can be an important means of self-expression.

Microphones

Real or play microphones are an outstanding way to play with sound. Teach the apraxic child to make sounds and to sing or talk into a microphone. Amplified speech, especially a child's own speech, usually attracts his attention and keeps him focused on sound production. Use a Megamike™, an Echomic™, a Rock-n-Roll Microphone™, a "jam box" with microphone and amplifier, a stereo system, an Auditory Trainer™, or a Phonic Ear™.

Chapter Three

The Power of Crowd Noise

Most nonverbal and minimally verbal young apraxic children will not speak on demand. When asked, "What's your name?" or when told to say, "ball," severely apraxic children often respond to these directives with silence, staring, ignoring, turning away, or simply refusing. Sometimes, it seems as if they aren't listening, have no idea what was said, or are determined not to speak. We often hear the parents of young apraxic children say, "He can say some things, but he just won't talk." Or, "He used to say some words, but doesn't anymore." Does this make sense? Why would a child who can make sounds or words not say them when asked?

Piaget observed that babies make lots of sounds when engulfed in crowd noise. He called this process *vocal contagion*. Vocal contagion is the natural urge to speak that spreads in highly verbal environments. For example, in busy places like shopping malls, babies who are wheeled from one end to the other tend to increase vocalization. Babies seem to enjoy matching their voices to the sounds of the people around them. The story of Sara will bring some clarity.

Sara

One day, two of my old friends came over with their five-month-old baby girl, Sara. The mother proceeded to place the child on a couch and prop her up into a sitting position with pillows.

Sara sat contentedly as we adults began to talk. Since we had not seen each other for over a year, there was a lot of excited talk about the changes our lives had taken. All of us seemed to talk at once until a little crowd noise had been generated.

After about fifteen minutes of our chatter, baby Sara began to coo and goo and make generally happy baby noises as she looked around the room and sucked on her hand. In my enthusiasm, I said, "Sara's talking." at which point all the adults stopped talking and looked to Sara. What do you think Sara did? She became quiet, of course, and stared happily back at us. We began to encourage her to talk by saying, "Talk, Sara, talk," and, "Hi Sara. Hi Sara," and several other silly things adults often say to get babies to talk on demand. Sara remained silent throughout our attempts as she smiled back at us with her big brown eyes.

After a few minutes, we adults lost interest in the baby and resumed our lively discussion. Again, Sara began to make sounds and again I stopped the group to direct them to Sara, who promptly stopped vocalizing again. This happened several times. Each time Sara vocalized contentedly during the crowd noise and stopped immediately when we stopped talking to listen to her. It was as if we had a switch with which to turn her vocalizations on and off at will.

Sara was right in the middle of the stage of vocal contagion. She was vocal when our speech filled the room, but was silent when there was general silence and attention was directed toward her. This is the dominant pattern in infants under six months of age who are developing normally, and it also controls the vocalizations of the young apraxic child who is stuck in the first stage of imitation development.

Vocal Contagion and the Apraxic Child

Apraxic children who are stuck in the first stage of imitation often make the most sound when they are free to vocalize in noisy conditions. Similarly, they are much less responsive when asked to speak on demand. It can be very frustrating for all involved with an apraxic child whose vocalizations are tied to crowd noise. For example, a classroom teacher often misses the fleeting spontaneous utterances of the apraxic child who produces them during the bustle of a highly verbal time in a classroom. She is simply too busy attending to everyone and everything to hear the unexpected and often difficult utterances of the apraxic child. Then, at a time when the classroom is quiet and she is ready to hear each child speak individually, the apraxic child probably will not speak up. Teachers often get the impression that the child could talk if he wanted to, and they begin to view the apraxic child as stubborn, uncooperative, or stupid, rather than disabled.

Using Vocal Contagion to Develop Imitation

Supports my of skills & play therapy

We can use the concept of vocal contagion to stimulate early imitation skill in children with severe childhood apraxia by providing a variety of vocally contagious environments and situations conducive to spontaneous sound and word utterances. The idea is to provide the child with opportunities to participate in a vocally contagious activity and carefully monitor the child's responses.

Two classic examples occurred many years ago when I was conducting preschool therapy at the University of Illinois.

Baby Doll Activity

In the classroom, eight or nine children, each three to five years of age, were seated around two tables. Each child had a baby doll and a doll blanket. I sat among the children with my own doll and blanket at one of the tables. As the children began to explore their items, I began to make simple comments about my baby. "My baby is sleeping." I said, and, "Night-night baby." The classroom was a mix of verbal, minimally verbal, and nonverbal children. The verbal ones chimed in right away with comments about what their babies were doing and what they were doing with their babies. "I'm changing my baby's diaper," one said. "My baby's hungry," said another.

I purposefully did not respond specifically to the children's utterances, nor did I ask any of the children questions, tell them what to say, or try to create a dialogue with any of them. Instead, I made general comments about my baby to the group. The result was that all the verbal children and I began to chime in about our babies, speaking up freely and simultaneously about our play. We were creating a small crowd-noise experience.

Within a few minutes, the nonverbal and minimally verbal apraxic children began to participate by making noises, saying single words like "baby" and "night-night" and generally joining in. Once the noise began, I continued my own comments to help sustain the level of crowd noise, hoping that the kids would keep going for at least fifteen minutes. The kids all dove in to the fun. The activity lasted about forty minutes. At times, many children echoed each other's utterances. After one child said, "I'm feeding my baby," four or five of the children began almost immediately to feed their babies and to say, "I'm feeding my baby." This spontaneous imitation of each other dominated the group many times.

We also engaged in chanting together about our babies with many two-word combinations like "baby eat" and "baby up" and "bye baby" as we played. Sometimes we sang parts of songs together. The songs were not lead or taught, just hummed or spoken in fragments and phrases. All in all, there was a tremendous amount of expressive speech and language emanating from that room as the apraxic children joined in the crowd noise.

Preston

At five years of age, Preston was described by his family as "not talking" and was enrolled in our preschool for children with speech and language delay or disorder. Preston seemed very bright, but even after several months in the program, he would not speak when spoken to, would not answer questions, and would not imitate any words on demand. Any connected speech he offered that we happened to hear during unstructured child-directed play time was unintelligible and seemed like jargon. We wondered whether or not it was real speech.

I worked with Preston's classroom teacher to create a vocally contagious environment as a means to get him to produce more spontaneous speech. This task was easy to accomplish in his classroom because his teacher was a musician and highly expressive, one who allowed the children what might be considered as too much expressive freedom. They had fun in there!

The teacher, Dave, set up a clay activity. He placed a huge mound of gray clay in the center of a fairly large round table with chairs. The kids simply were to play there, a class of approximately 15 children. Preston was just one of the crowd. Dave sat to the side and played his guitar, making up songs about the children's creations as they unfolded. The children had no boundaries on what they could say or how they could say it. The only rule was to stay at the table and play with the clay.

The activity started out as most do, with the children hesitantly picking out pieces of clay and beginning the process of rolling, squeezing, poking, and shaping. As the minutes ticked by, and the clay got warmer and more pliable, the children began to make comments about their clay creations and Dave began to sing about them. "Oh!" Dave sang, "Robbie's making a snake; and Julie's making a car; and Carrie, she's making something big; and Jake's making something small!" The songs continued. The children began to talk about what they were doing. Preston sat silently poking at his clay.

Gently, after ten or fifteen minutes of play, Preston began to say something. I couldn't hear him, because the din had grown, but I could see his lips moving. He was holding up his wad of clay as if he were showing it to someone. No one paid attention because everyone was doing something different, so Preston went back to his clay.

A few minutes later, the same thing occurred: Preston said something and held up his clay. This time the teacher saw him and looked to me for what to do. I shook my head and indicated that the teacher should ignore him. The teacher asked, "Are you sure?"

I said, "Yes." Again Preston sat down and went back to his work.

The same thing happened again a few minutes later, and again several minutes later, and then again and again, over and over. Each time Preston got louder and more enthusiastic about showing his work and saying something about it until, at one point, he practically got up on the table to show his clay and shouted something that all could hear. Now, the teacher could not hold back and said, "Great job, Preston!" and went back to his song.

For the rest of the hour-long activity, Preston continued to talk out, telling the group about what he was doing. We could not understand anything he said, but it was his free expression to join the group. We all came to know that Preston could talk quite a bit under the right conditions, and I began to understand how I could help him imitate by continuing to use vocal contagion with crowd noise to get the process going.

When therapists or teachers ask me what they can do in the classroom to encourage expressive speech and language skills with

children, I tell them to set up a vocally contagious situation and teach the children to join in on the sounds and words as they occur. These activities and hundreds of others like them have taught me the therapeutic power of crowd noise for the severely apraxic child. Apraxic children speak up the most when in a group that is singing, reciting together, or calling out things to teachers and to one another.

Crowd Noise Power Centers

The following suggestions will help you see this process in everyday experiences and find ways to add this element to your treatment of apraxic children.

Playground

On the playground, adults should worry less about the apraxic child's communication with others and more about the child's ability to join in the wild and mostly uncontrolled vocal and verbal play. Encourage the child to laugh, scream, shout, squeal, yell, call, sing, and to say "Oooooo! Eeeeee! Ahhhhhh!" and, "Ohhhhhhh!" as he moves on and around the gross motor equipment.

Gross Motor Play

Small or large occupational or physical therapy sessions, adapted PE classes, and some gymnastics and swimming classes are good places to stimulate vocal contagion. These are times to play on balls, trampolines, and climbing structures; in and out of crawling tubes; in water; on mats; and so forth. Create storylines the children can follow in their play. For example, pretend the beanbag chairs are mountains and the tubes are train tunnels. Let the imagination flow and let the small-group play begin!

Proprioceptive Hand Play

The term *proprioceptive hand play* refers to those activities that require the hands to move in large movement patterns, such as playing with Playdough, clay, or mud. Although a child can engage in these activities at any time, a group can be used to make the activity vocally contagious.

Tactile Hand Play

Tactile hand play refers to activities that require the hands to move in and around substances that are highly stimulating to the skin, such as sand, water, fingerpaints, shaving cream, beans, rice, buttons, hand lotion, and so forth. As always, a group is needed in order to make the activity vocally contagious.

Story Time

While story time is usually a sustained quiet period for children, it also can be an excellent time to create a vocally contagious environment. For example, the story of Goldilocks and the Three Bears can be interrupted at times with growls, "Ooo's," and "Ahhh's."

Singing

Probably the best way to stimulate crowd noise in a classroom setting is to lead activities in which the children respond together in song—a natural stimulator of vocal contagion. Lead a variety of songs, but be mindful that those with repeatable words or stanzas will benefit apraxic children the most. For example, the "Alphabet Song" and "Happy Birthday" have stanzas that repeat.

Chanting

Chanting is another powerful type of crowd noise. In chanting, the same sound, word, or phrase is repeated simultaneously by the entire group of children. My baby doll activity described above was a perfect chanting activity that included many rote words and phrases, like, "My baby's hungry," and, "My baby's cold." It is far better for an apraxic child to succeed in saying the same thing multiple times than to fail at saying something new.

Chapter Four

Creating One Voice for
Imitation Development

Now you know that babies under six months of age will vocalize to themselves to experience the sensorimotor aspects of varying sounds and they like to join into ambient crowd noise. In addition, babies can make sounds that coordinate one-on-one with a single voice. This is called *vocal synchrony*, another powerful tool for imitation development. Vocal synchrony teaches a child how other people can sound like him. With this skill, the apraxic child is better equipped to understand how he can sound like other people.

Performing in synchrony means that two or more people do the same thing at the same time, such as synchronized swimmers who perform uniform acrobatics in the water. When a child joins the sound of a crowd, he makes sound in synchrony with the ambient noises around him—excellent for gross speech participation. But an even more refined practice of speech sound discrimination and production occurs when a baby vocalizes in synchrony with one other voice in a face-to-face interaction.

For example, a content baby will coo throughout a typical day. The parents sometimes join in and coo with him, or talk to him in soothing ways using words with similar lilting tones: "You are such a good baby," and, "Hi, my sweet little man. I hear you talking to me. Yes, I do. I hear you."

Research has indicated that parents who are good language models, especially mothers, do this automatically as a part of what has been called *motherese*—the language of mothers to their babies. Speaking to the child in a way that matches the child's voice gives the child and his parent a crystal clear moment of coordinated speech interaction that is pleasurable to both child and adult. This creates a joint vocalization experience that is richer and fuller than a solo voice.

Singers and musicians are experts of synchronistic vocal and instrumental productions. When two singers perform synchronous tones, the sound surpasses what one person could do alone with intensity, pitch, loudness, length, and vibrato. Tone and overtones are created. When one party begins to shift the sound, the other follows in order to maintain the synchrony.

The only way an infant and an adult can make synchronistic vocal productions is if the adult makes the sounds the baby is making. If the child is cooing and the adult makes sounds or words with the same vocal quality, a synchronistic vocal experience will be created. However, if the adult ignores what the child is saying and tries to get him to say something else, vocal synchrony will fail. The baby who is truly operating in the stage of vocal contagion will not be able to imitate the adult's new model, because he does not have that kind of control over his own voice yet.

The rehearsal of synchronistic vocalizations is the most sophisticated ingredient we have discussed so far in early imitation development. This is how children discover that sounds produced by two different people can match. This is a primary tool in developing speech and imitation skills from this point forward.

Vocal Synchrony and the Apraxic Child

Vocal synchrony is a skill lacking in most severely apraxic children. Some engage in the process while others do not. Some get stuck in this stage while others never enter it. Because so many apraxic children produce so few vocalizations, many of them have not had the opportunity to engage in vocal synchrony for extended periods of time. Thus, they have not learned the auditory and vocal skills that can be gained through the process. As a result, apraxic children typically develop significantly less conceptual skill regarding the discrimination of their own vocal sounds and have poorly developed skills to compare their own productions to those of others. In fact, the idea of producing the same sound as another person has not occurred to many of them.

To compound the issue, most adults do not naturally engage in vocal synchrony with children beyond the infant and early toddler years. Since childhood apraxia typically is not detected or even suspected until these children are at least two years of age or older, most parents, teachers, and therapists don't consider employing vocal synchrony as part of their repertoire of stimulation techniques. Thus, many apraxic children receive absolutely no experience with this foundational level of imitation skill. When asked to, "Say, 'ball,'" the young apraxic child fails because he has not learned how his vocalizations relate to those of others, let alone how to match that particular sequence of sounds.

of course!

dat

Vocal Synchrony As a Tool in Therapy

Vocal synchrony is easy to use with an apraxic child. This kind of imitation draws the child out of himself and into better alignment with what is being said. The child becomes more in tune with speech from others when that speech is in tune with his. It's one of the oldest rules of language therapy: Begin where the child is functioning and draw him out from there.

Vocal synchrony requires no special materials, lesson plans, or extra work by the child. The adults do the work. As a therapy technique, we can simply apply it to the way we regularly talk to apraxic children during treatment activities or daily routines. The process requires that we simply imitate the child's spontaneous vocalizations while he is in the process of making them.

Guidelines

The following guidelines can be used with an apraxic child who is minimally verbal and operating at the earliest stages of imitation. These guidelines can help you understand how to engage in vocal synchrony in tandem with other treatment activities.

PROVIDE AN ENVIRONMENT THAT IS FREE FROM PRESSURE TO TALK

Don't ask the child questions or put him in a situation that will pressure him to respond. Be patient and wait for his spontaneous vocal productions and then imitate them.

Work closely face-to-face

Synchrony is best achieved in a fairly close, face-to-face work setting called *mutual gazing.* This can be accomplished in any position (sitting, lying prone or supine, etc.) and with any props, as long as you and the child are working near one another. A pair of fake glasses with a funny nose and mustache is a neat trick to draw the child's face and gaze toward you. Also, use hand cues near your mouth to draw the child's attention to your face and mouth, or hold toys the child wants next to your mouth so that he sees your face as he makes sounds of desire.

Do not make mutual gazing a prerequisite

Don't worry about face-to-face communication if you can't get it. A child does not have to be gazing in an adult's face in order to hear the sounds she is producing and engage in vocal synchrony. Many apraxic, dysarthric, and autistic patients have been treated just fine without mutual gazing. You can play with toys together and vocalize without looking at one another. Over time, you'll find new ways to attract the child's eyes. Sometimes a puppet with a wide mouth is an excellent substitute for face-to-face work. Other options include a mirror or a partially reflecting window.

Try to sound exactly like the child

The more your voice sounds like the child's, the quicker he will hear the synchrony and get the idea. When he says "weee!" on the swing, do the same. Match it by pitch, loudness, intonation, length, resonance, and vowel sound. Shift your voice with the child.

Synchronize inhalation and exhalation patterns

Inhale as the child inhales and exhale as the child exhales. If the child gasps for air between productions, do the same with him. Try to anticipate when he will begin and end a sound. Then vocalize just as he does. Do the same by playing horns, whistles, sirens, and kazoos. The closer you get to matching the apraxic child's inhalation and exhalation patterns, the more vocally synchronous you will be.

Don't worry about specific consonants, vowels, or words

Imitate what the child says without worrying about whether you are making specific consonants, vowels, or words. The idea is for you to get the child to pay attention to what he is already doing. Remember, at this level you are only trying to get him to play with sound, not to work with it. Synchronistic vocalizations are your goal, your means, and your end.

IMITATE SEVERAL TIMES PER DAY FOR SHORT PERIODS

At home, it is best to imitate the child many times per day for short periods of time, instead of trying to do it all at once. Five interactions per day is plenty. Each one can last less than a minute.

ONCE SYNCHRONICITY OCCURS REGULARLY, TRY TO MAKE IT LAST

Turn a ten-second synchronistic production into a twenty-second one. Turn three minutes of synchronistic vocal play into five minutes. The longer synchronicity takes place during each individual synchronistic moment, the further your child will go in developing this early speech-imitation skill.

TAKE BREAKS AT HOME

A parent should not engage in synchronistic vocal productions all day long. If you do, you may create a child who expects a response to his every utterance. You do not want that to occur. You both need time away from each other, even if you are in the same room. Also, build in times when you expect the child to be quiet, like when you're in a grocery store or restaurant.

DO IT ALL THE TIME IN THERAPY

Unlike a parent's responsibility at home, a therapist can freely engage in vocal synchrony for every moment of each individual therapy session. Once or twice per week of uninterrupted vocal synchrony will greatly benefit the child.

ALLOW TIMES FOR SELF-TALK

Most young children enjoy self-talk as they play alone. The child should begin the process of self-talk early and sustain it throughout the entire course of treatment. Provide times during the day when he plays alone with his toys and is free to talk to himself. Note: This is not TV time. Television encourages children to be quiet and watch, not to vocalize.

Therapists can include self-talk time during treatment as well. When I am treating a child who is stimulated to begin self-talk, I remain quiet so he can work through it. It's good for him. During this time, I monitor what he is saying and how he says it, and I may take a language sample or make notes about the child's phonetic or phonological development. When he winds down, I may begin the process again or move to other aspects of the program.

Do not overstimulate the child

Some children will get wound up during vocal synchrony and lose their ability to get focused and quiet again. Therapists must assess how much vocal synchrony to use to get the child vocal without being overstimulated, and then work within that time frame. Some children need an absolutely silent time to calm down before being dismissed from therapy or moving on to other activities. Others may need a large-motor activity to burn off steam before they can come down from the vocal heights. Some children like the wild and out-of-control feeling they get from vocal synchrony and may need to be told firmly to settle down. If the child is out of control, he won't process as well. The goal is to stimulate the auditory and vocal system to the point where it can be used to stimulate vocal productions and synchronistic vocal imitations. If the child is moving beyond that, he is being overstimulated and the technique is no longer useful for him.

Monitor the child's vocalizations over time

In speech and language therapy, vocal synchrony can be used as a primary tool for almost any length of time. Ask yourself: Does the process of vocal synchrony seem to be stimulating the child to be more vocal during both therapy and non-therapy times? It should over time. Continue to engage in the process as long as the child is demonstrating benefit from it. As characteristics of the next stage of imitation begin to emerge, begin to fade out vocal synchrony.

Use a log or journal

Parents or teachers may need a written record of their synchronistic interactions with their child to better analyze the process and keep track of what they are doing. Entries can be brief.

Although keeping a log of vocal behaviors may be the last thing a busy parent wants to do, it can help them see the process at work and keep it going. It also lets the therapist know how much the parents are doing at home. After a few weeks, or even just a few days, most families can discontinue the log because they will see the effects and will automatically engage in the process without prompts or reminders.

DON'T BE AFRAID TO USE REAL WORDS

This entire process can and should be done with sounds as well as real words, especially if your child already has begun to use them. Use words, phrases, nursery rhymes, silly sayings, songs, rote counting, the ABCs, or anything else that sparks your child's interest for sustaining synchronistic interactions with you. Remember, your goal is to match your child's voice in as many ways as possible.

BE PATIENT

Some people might feel silly when beginning the process of engaging in vocal synchrony by imitating a child's spontaneous productions. They might think they aren't doing anything, because they aren't trying to get the child to say anything new. Speech and language pathologists as well parents can begin to be impatient about the process or anxious about moving on to more advanced stages. Everything in us cries out to model new sounds and words for the child to say!

But the severely apraxic child is not ready for that level of language stimulation. If he were, he would imitate all the sounds and words you modeled for him. To get through this, it always helps to remember the baby. This therapy provides the apraxic child the tools he needs to get ready to imitate speech. Be patient and watch the process unfold.

Chapter Five

Laughter Encourages Turn Taking

Communication is a back-and-forth exchange between two or more people, a process we call *turn taking*. For example, when we meet a friend and say "Hi!" we take the first turn to talk. When our friend says something back, he is making a response. Then when we say, "What are you doing?" we are taking a subsequent turn. And so it goes.

Turn taking is a foundational skill in imitation development. A modeled sound or word is a first turn, and a child's imitation of it is a second turn. Although babies in the first stage of imitation development can synchronize their voices with others, they do not take turns, except in one area: laughter. Laughter is integral to both speech and expressive language development.

Babies begin to smile at about two months of age. Between two and six months of age they chortle, giggle, chuckle, and eventually begin to laugh out loud. It is almost impossible not to giggle along with them. Happy babies can change even our grumpiest mood. Also, by identifying the things they see as funny—exaggerated faces, actions, gestures, and interesting sounds or words—babies give clues about their intelligence. Sometimes it is surprising what makes a particular baby laugh, but when he does, most adults take note of the circumstance and proceed to reenact it in order to get the child to laugh again.

Special Properties of Laughter

Laughter is an incredibly important step in the development of imitation skill because of its special properties: access, energy, stamina, imitation, and family cohesiveness.

Access

Often, laughter is the very first thing adults can do to get a specific and consistent response from their child. We cannot make babies produce any other sound during the earliest stage of imitation development, but we can make them laugh. Laughter is a powerful tool in the process of learning to imitate speech because it can be used to generate sound.

Energy

Other than crying, laughter is the first sound a baby produces with great energy. Other sounds produced in this early period are vocalized rather softly, with little force or energy. High-energy laughter draws the baby's attention to his own physical sensations and encourages diaphragm exercise.

Stamina

Laughter is the longest sound produced by an infant who is under six months of age. Therefore, it is a principle sound for teaching a baby how to sustain an exhale while phonating. These prolonged vocalizations help build stamina in diaphragm contraction and help to build progressively longer syllable sequences. Over the long haul, this work builds a foundation for the prolonged phonation needed for babbling, multi-syllabic words, and two- and three-word combinations.

Imitation

When a baby finds something funny and laughs, almost everyone else around him responds with laughter. The adults and other children that may ignore his other tiny sounds almost never ignore his laughter. This demonstrates to the infant how people imitate one another. The intensity of the joint laughter routine draws the child's attention outside of himself and directs it to the actions, gestures, vocalizations, and words of others. It is a key to learning to imitate in turn, and the infant learns powerful lessons about grouping similar sounds.

Family Cohesiveness

A baby's laughter and a family's response increase group cohesiveness. In some families, a baby's laughter is the first event that coerces the whole family into accepting the child as a full member of the clan. Before laughter, babies can seem uninvolved and self-centered—which they are. His laughter marks his first substantial contribution to the family. Most families are relieved when their baby begins to laugh, because it makes them feel good and it makes the family look good.

Laughter and the Child with Childhood Apraxia

It may surprise many readers to realize that significant numbers of young children with severe childhood apraxia do not laugh. Some squeal and others squeak or sniff, but few laugh. While squeaking, squealing, and sniffing are valuable pre-speech behaviors, laughter is the vocalization that is most important for imitative development because of the special properties described above. Apraxic children who don't laugh can miss the positive benefits that typical babies gain.

Lack of laughter . . .

- Leaves adults without an easy tool for eliciting sound from their apraxic child
- Deprives the apraxic child of the diaphragm exercise he needs for the production of prolonged sound
- Leaves the apraxic child without the high-energy, non-stressful tool he needs for drawing other's attention to him
- Impairs the apraxic child's ability to attend to the tactile and proprioceptive sensations of powerful vocalization
- Prevents others from laughing back along with the child, which fails to provide him with reciprocal turn-taking models of vocalization
- Increases the perception that the apraxic child is not contributing to the happiness and well-being of the family unit

- In social situation—like, in the classroom—may perpetuate feelings in others that the apraxic child is not involved and is not contributing to the larger social group, thus less social turn taking may occur

Speech and language pathologists, parents, and other members of service provider teams are asked to take a good look at their apraxic children and ask, "Does he laugh out loud?" Children who do laugh should engage in laughter routines to increase their cognitive awareness and voluntary control of it. Children who do not laugh need help to develop this important vocal and imitative skill. Laughter makes therapy fun, and it takes very little planning. When laughter is used in this way, reluctant clients are "tricked" into vocalizing. Plus, they usually do not rebuke treatment, because nothing unpleasant or impossible is demanded from them. Laughter can be elicited any time of the day or evening, under any circumstances, in any position, and with any props. The only work is to discover what gets the child to laugh and then to use it to engage in vocal synchrony. Laughter will help your apraxic child begin the process of turn taking in imitation.

Before we list the guidelines for using laughter in therapy, the following describes how laughter was used with one five-year-old child with severe childhood apraxia.

Shamus

Shamus was five years of age, nonverbal, and would say only two vowel sounds spontaneously. These could not be elicited by any means, and he did not imitate any other sounds that I could determine. Shamus was neurologically impaired, hearing impaired, and generally self-absorbed and engaged in self-stimulating activity. He also demonstrated severe tactile defensive behavior. Shamus gagged easily when touched anywhere around the face, neck, or upper body, and he had highly selective food preferences.

I had to find some way to reach this child, to draw him out of himself into a broader world where he could begin to pay attention and imitate. I began to work with his tactile system early in therapy. He was severely hypersensitive, so I hoped it would have a positive effect on his expressive vocalizations and imitation.

Early in treatment I sat on the floor across from him at a small table. Shamus sat and played with an assortment of toys. With his mother's permission, I began to squeeze his feet, then his ankles, then his calves, then his knees, then his thighs, moving slowly toward his hips, trunk, upper body, and head. I discovered right away that when I held his calves, knees, and thighs firmly, he began to wiggle and squirm and laugh hysterically. Discovery! By applying careful deep pressure to his calves, knees, and thighs, I could get him to laugh! Now I had a way to elicit sound from Shamus without waiting for him to imitate me.

By laughing along with him, I was able to develop joint laughter routines and vocal synchrony. Within weeks, this lead to synchronistic experimentations with the basic parameters of sound—voice, pitch, loudness, prolongation, and vowel. Within five months, Shamus began to experiment enough with these features of speech that his productions began to sound like pre-speech behavior. Miraculously, he tried some simple words and phrases. Within six months, we were recognizing many spontaneous words, such as *I want, yea, no, this,* and *that.*

Getting Kids to Laugh

Everyone knows how to make children laugh. The following guidelines are offered simply as a list of perspectives for using laughter in your setting, be it home, classroom, or therapy center.

Create the Right Setting

Drawing laughter from an apraxic child is more art than science. It requires finding that playful place within ourselves in which we connect with children and create a light atmosphere. Silly puppets are one of my easiest avenues, and I like to work physically close.

But some apraxic children don't like this kind of play and only laugh under certain conditions. One two-year-old, severely apraxic child only laughed when he discovered that out of sight did not mean out of mind. He thought this was the funniest thing in the world and giggled every time I hid an object behind my back or under the table. Another five-year-old laughed only when my hand puppet "ate" plastic food. He fed that puppet for more than twenty minutes in individual sessions and laughed every time it chomped down on the plastic delights. Every therapist, teacher, and parent must explore their own play skills and discover the events that create an atmosphere of fun for the child.

Find a Tickle Spot and Procedure

Tickling is one of the easiest methods of encouraging laughter. Common tickle spots include tummies, shoulders, under-the-chin, armpits, the back, feet, calves, ears, and the nape of the neck. Any place that causes your child to react with laughter is a tickle spot. Also, determine what type of tickling elicits the response. Is it light touch or deep pressure? Experiment to find what causes your child to laugh best.

Honor the Child's Reaction

Some children do not find tickling funny at all. In fact, they fear it. Stop tickling immediately if a child shows a strong negative response, such as hitting, biting, moving away, crying, or saying "Don't!" These reactions may seem too strong for the amount of sensory stimuli you are providing, but remember, many of these children perceive incoming tactile and proprioceptive sensations differently than we do. What may seem like fun to us may be perceived as pain or may be confusing to an apraxic child. This is especially important when there is a history of neglect or abuse, or when a child has tactile hypersensitivity, vestibular dysfunction, poor balance reactions, disorientation, or recruitment of sensation.

If tickling causes discomfort or pain in your client and he begins to avoid it, refuse it, or act out, discontinue its use immediately. You do not want to put a wedge between the two of you simply because the technique works easily with other apraxic children, and you do not want to further disorient your client. Very light tickle procedures seem to be accepted more readily by most of these children, including barely touching or blowing on the skin of the back, neck, chin, sternum, or ears.

Be Patient

You may not elicit laughter right away in some of the most severely apraxic children. Some of these children will hold their breath or squeal for quite some time, rather than laugh. Include laughter here and there at home and in therapy to monitor its development. When a child begins a real laugh, begin to use it more often to exercise its function. Most parents will find it such a relief that their child can finally laugh—even though they may not have realized that it was absent earlier—that they will be willing to facilitate laughter often at home. An entire speech therapy session spent in laughter can be good when a child is first engaging in vocal synchrony! Laughter is a key to getting the child to vocalize.

Protect Yourself

It is important to realize that tickling is not a standard traditional speech and language therapy technique, nor even a well-known technique for developing imitation in apraxic children. Protect yourself by making sure that parents, colleagues, and administrators receive information about this method. Also, consider having parents give their written permission for this hands-on approach. You do not want to be accused of touching a child for questionable reasons.

yep! Too bad.

Laugh with the Child

Create a synchronistic atmosphere by laughing along with the child. Try to imitate his laughter in terms of voice, intonation, breath patterns, and loudness.

Use Laughter to Get a Response

The whole point of using laughter in the facilitation of imitation development is to teach turn taking. Thus, you want to structure your interaction with the child in such a way that the process of initiating and responding will become obvious. When tickling, create an atmosphere of great anticipation and wait for the child's strong laughter response. By working back and forth in this way, we can create an atmosphere of turn taking by using the simple sound of laughter.

Chapter Six

Learning to Take Turns in Dialogue

Once the basics of imitation development have been learned, including sound, crowd noise, synchrony, and laughter, a baby graduates into a new stage of imitation development that Piaget entitled *mutual imitation.*

Mutual imitation is all about dialogue. The term *dialogue* refers to the back-and-forth or turn-taking nature of communication between two people. The root words *di* and *logo* mean "two" and "word," respectfully. Directly translated, *dialogue* means "two words," or words emanating from two sources. In today's culture, dialogue is understood to mean more than words, but sounds, gestures, and facial expressions as well.

Dialogues between people follow several basic rules. The following represents part of a dialogue between two verbal adult women who are mothers of school-age children just back from camp. Our two players, Mary and Karen, chance to meet at a neighborhood grocery store. Mary's utterances appear in the left-hand column and Karen's on the right. Read through the dialogue line by line, from left to right. Read it carefully before reading about the rules below. For future reference, this segment is called the Camping Dialogue.

Camping Dialogue

Mary	Karen
Hi.	Hey!
How are you?	Fine, thanks, how are things at your house?
Great. My kids are back from camp.	Oh, yea. How did they like it?
Well, I think they had a great time.	I heard someone else say it was really good this year.
I think it was. They all said they want to go back next year. . . .	

Basic Rules of Dialogue Construction

When we look carefully at the individual utterances within the Camping Dialogue, we see that it is constructed following a few basic rules.

1. Dialogues consist of back-and-forth turns that extend over a period of time.
2. Dialogues contain initiation turns.
3. Dialogues contain response turns.
4. Dialogues conclude with an ending turn. (In the sample, the ellipses [. . .] indicates that the dialogue continued.)

Even the simplest of exchanges follow these basic rules. Consider the following brief dialogue between two seventh grade boys who have been sitting silently next to one another while waiting for their bus after school. Although compact, this dialogue also follows these rules.

MATT	DYLAN
See ya'.	Later.
Yea.	

This rudimentary yet typical exchange follows all of our rules. There are turns, both initiation and response, and there is an ending.

A dialogue exists between two people no matter how long or short it is and regardless of how many or how few words are used. Dialogue does not occur, however, when a person is alone or when a speech is broadcast on the television or radio. Those are called *monologues*. Dialogue requires the interaction of at least two people.

Why are we concerned about the rules of dialogue formation in our discussion of imitation development in severely apraxic children? Think about it: When we model a sound or word for an apraxic child to imitate, we become the initiator in a dialogue. We expect the child to respond in turn. Sounds and words are imitated within the context of dialogues. Children with childhood apraxia must learn to participate in dialogue in order to learn to imitate through it. Before we discuss dialogue participation among apraxic children, however, let's take a close look at early dialogue routines in infants.

Emerging Dialogue in Infancy

By six months of age, little babies begin to use their vocal skills to participate in dialogues with those around them, and these primitive dialogues follow the same basic rules described above. The following represents a typical dialogue from this stage of development. It is a primitive conversation between a six-month-old baby girl named Jessica and her mother. Please read it carefully left to right, and refer back to it throughout the rest of our discussion. For future reference we shall call it the Jessica Dialogue.

Jessica Dialogue

JESSICA	MOTHER
[Making happy baby sounds.]	[Changing diaper.] Hi sweetie, are you a good baby? [Pause.]
Oooo. Oooo.	Oooo. I love you. [Pause.]
[Raspberry.]	Is that so? That' s a funny sound. [Pause.]
[Smile.]	That' s a funny sound. [Bends down close to child. Pause.]
[Smiling, reaches to Mom' s face.]	Momma. [Pause.]
[Touches mom' s nose.]	Nose. That' s Momma' s nose. [Pause.]
[Raspberry.]	That' s my nose.
[Raspberry.]	[Raspberry.] [Pause.]
[Raspberry.]	[Raspberry.]
Ooooo.	Nose. Can you say "nose"? [Pause.]
[Smile.]	[Finishes diapering.] There you go. [Puts child down on blanket.]

Can't you just imagine this mother and her baby communicating in this way as your read each turn? It demonstrates a classic interaction between a baby who is both interactive and vocal, and a mother who is using motherese to create a dialogue with her baby. Does this exchange satisfy our basic rules of dialogue formation? Let's question each aspect.

1. Is there a sequence of turns? Yes, the mother and baby communicate in sequence.
2. Is there an initiation turn? Yes, the "happy baby sounds" initiate the first turn.
3. Are there response turns? Yes, from each party.
4. Is there a back-and-forth nature defined by the turns? Yes, the exchange continues throughout.
5. Is there an ending turn? Yes, the mother ends the exchange by putting the baby down and saying, "There you go."

A baby begins to develop communication routines by participating in primitive dialogues. As the child and his parents exchange comments, gestures, facial expressions, sounds, and eventually words, the baby learns how these turns are related to one another. In its most mature form, imitation is the process of relating speech sounds and words to one another over time. It requires awareness of other people, the ability to pay attention to them, and patience to wait one's turn in the exchange. Imitation evolves from a sequential exchange in dialogue.

Dialogue in Apraxic Children

Children with childhood apraxia often respond in silence to requests for imitation. A typical interaction with a nonverbal apraxic child might look like this:

Adult	Child
Can you say "boat"?	[Silence.]

In this case, the adult initiates with a carrier phrase and a target word, and the child responds with silence. The child does not say the target word and does not take his turn in the dialogue exchange. In the Jessica Dialogue, did you notice that even though the six-month-old baby couldn't say words or imitate the mother's sounds, she did take her turn in the dialogue? She has learned the framework and soon will be able to deposit sounds and words.

Severely apraxic children rarely respond when asked to speak. However, the spontaneous things they say can be treated as initiation turns. These are what I call *one-step dialogues.* For example:

Child	Adult
Truck.	Truck. You have a truck.
[Silence.]	

Exchanges like these are the beginnings of dialogue because the adult makes them so, not because the child did anything to create a dialogue. The child merely named the object. It is my experience that these one-step dialogues dominate the conversational skills of the youngster with apraxia.

Without turn taking no real imitation skills can develop. If a child only makes spontaneous utterances and does not say things in sequence with others, then the child will never imitate another's utterance promptly. The child may imitate sounds or words he heard some time earlier, but he will never be able to practice words repeatedly within the frame of a dialogue, which is the essence of speech maturation and speech correction.

Engaging a young apraxic child in dialogue can be frustrating. At this level, he does not recognize the back-and-forth nature of dialogue and the fundamental process of taking turns. In order to teach him to imitate we must first teach him how to take turns within a dialogue frame.

Rules for Developing Primitive Dialogue

There are four simple rules to follow when helping a young apraxic child develop a dialogue frame.

1. Allow the child to be the initiator.
2. Be a responder.
3. Give the turn back to the child with a silent pause.
4. Allow the child to say anything for his turn.

We shall describe each of these rules as it applies directly to the apraxic child. The Jessica Dialogue is rich with information about how to use these rules. Refer back to it as each rule is explained.

Allow the Child to Be the Initiator

The first and foremost rule of developing imitation skills in a young apraxic child goes contrary to every instinct we have about stimulating language development: Allow the child to be the initiator of the dialogue.

In the Jessica Dialogue, the mother did not get the baby to make sounds. The baby simply was making sounds at the moment in which the mother began to interact with her. Jessica did not intend her vocalizations to initiate dialogue, but Mom treated them as such. Most apraxic children are similar; they spontaneously make some sounds or words that are not necessarily intended to be initiations. A child's vocalization only becomes an initiation turn in a dialogue if the communication partner treats it that way.

Mothers and babies interact like this all the time as they talk to one another in bits and pieces of dialogue. Consciously or unconsciously, the mother knows that if she keeps this up, one day the child will say a real word in turn. You get a sense of this when the mother says, "Momma," or, "Nose. That's Momma's nose." She even says, "Nose. Can you say 'nose'?" The mother models these words to the child in the hopes that she will hear them repeated, but she does not allow the child's lack of imitation to interfere with her dialogue construction.

51

Treating spontaneous utterances as initiation turns is an idea of vast importance to our work with severely apraxic children. Begin listening to the sounds your child already produces and respond to them yourself. By allowing your child to be the initiator of the dialogue, you begin the process of creating dialogue frames. The following ideas will help you get started.

Note Your Child's Spontaneous Utterances

Begin to take stock of the sounds and words your child already says. Perhaps he laughs, grunts, makes raspberries, or says "momma" or "ahhh." Whatever your child says, this is where you begin. Do not expect your child to say anything new or anything that you model for him. It's too early for that. Instead, listen to the sounds or words your child produces spontaneously. These utterances will be the core elements to use in developing the dialogue.

Make a List

I always make lists of the sounds and words I hear my apraxic clients say, and I update them often. This is an effective technique to keep track of their vocal abilities and is an excellent way for parents to begin listening to their children. In the absence of real, intelligible words, parents often do not hear what the child says, because they have never been trained to do so. By recording these utterances, parents can train their ears to hear the child more effectively.

Honor Spontaneous Sounds and Words as Dialogue

Begin to think of everything the child says spontaneously as an initiation of dialogue. Then consider your role in the dialogue as a responder. The story of Danielle will help you understand this idea.

Danielle

Danielle was a five-year-old girl with severe childhood apraxia who was nonverbal and almost nonvocal. The only speech sound she made was a flat, low-pitched monotone production of "ah-dah," which she said often. For example, she said "ah-dah" when taking a toy, when pointing to a picture, or when handing over a toy. The family ignored this sound because they thought it had no use. Instead, they were trying to get her to say words like *hi* and *momma*.

I began to treat Danielle's sound as an initiation turn in a dialogue and responded to it as if she were saying a real word to me. It sounded something like "What's that?" so I treated it as such. For example, if she handed me a toy and said "ah-dah," I responded with, "What's that? Doll." I did this every time she made the sound and taught her mother to do it as well. Within six weeks, Danielle had increased the number of times per day that she said "ah-dah" so that the parents said they heard her say it "all the time." During individual therapy sessions, Danielle and I began to have one-step dialogues like this:

Danielle	Me
Ah-dah.	What' s that? Shoe.
[Silence.]	[Silence.]
Ah-dah.	What' s that? Car.
[Silence.]	[Silence.]
Ah-dah.	What' s that? Boat.
[Silence.]	[Silence.]
Ah-dah.	What' s that? Mommy.
[Silence.]	[Silence.]
Ah-dah.	What' s that? Daddy. . . .

I have had hundreds of conversations like this with young apraxic children. Without question, this is the way dialogue begins for them. For Danielle and for many others like her, these one-step dialogues teach the structure of the dialogue frame. Once the frame is ready, apraxic children can begin to take each step toward developing better imitation skills. These will be described in the next chapters.

Be a Responder

The second rule of dialogue formation is that the adult should play the responder role. If the adult consistently responds to the child's initiations of haphazard utterances, then the child receives confirmation of the dialogue process. In the Jessica Dialogue, the mother takes the responder role most of the time, which is what makes the baby's utterances part of a long dialogue. Without the mother's responses, a dialogue would not exist.

The following story of Stephanie demonstrates what can happen when parents do not know how to respond to a child who is developing normally in all other areas and has already begun to talk.

Stephanie

Stephanie was a two-year-old girl who was referred to me for evaluation of speech and language abilities by a physician. The parents reported that she had not begun to talk at all. The physician suspected that the child might be apraxic. I visited the family in their home, and both parents were present. They both insisted that Stephanie could not talk: "She has never said a thing," and, "Do you think she will ever talk?"

I watched the child carefully as she played at the coffee table in front of me, and I began to make an inventory of the spontaneous things she said while the parents and I talked.

The interesting thing about this first visit was that I heard Stephanie say at least ten different words during this hour. As she played alone, she said to herself, "hi," "no," "yea," "doll," "snake," "bye," "mine," "uh-uh," "uh-huh," "OK," and a few other things that were unintelligible to me. Each word was a spontaneous and unexpected utterance that she said quietly to herself. You could have easily missed any of these remarks. Never once during this hour did the parents indicate that they had heard her, nor did they respond to Stephanie even though she said several words multiple times. Instead, the parents asked her to say specific things for me. For example, "What's your name, Stephanie? Can you say your name? . . . How old are you, Stephanie? . . . Can you say 'Hi' to Pam?" Stephanie did not reply to any of these prompts. Because the parents were not listening to what Stephanie produced spontaneously, they concluded that she could not talk.

We began a yearlong process of therapy for Stephanie, meeting weekly for three months, followed by two meetings in six months, and then meeting again for five final sessions over a three-month period. During these sessions, I did nothing but play with Stephanie and respond to what she said spontaneously. I gradually taught her mother to do so as well. The mother began to listen and respond to what Stephanie was saying, and Stephanie gradually began talking more and with greater regularly. By the end, Stephanie had caught up with her peers and was speaking in sentences.

Stephanie showed no real evidence of childhood apraxia. Therefore, she should experience no lingering problems from this delayed onset of expressive speech and language. The process of responding to a child's spontaneous utterances can have a powerful impact on a child's ability to talk.

There are four basic ways in which we can respond to our children's spontaneous utterances in order to create a dialogue frame. We can use words, vocalizations, actions, and imitations of the child.

Words

Words are a common way adults create dialogue with babies and young children. In the Jessica Dialogue, Mom responds to her with many words, including: "Hi, sweetie. Are you a good baby?" and "Nose. That's momma's nose."

Words are a natural response when working with an apraxic child. For example, if an apraxic child reaches for a toy car and says, "Uh," an adult can respond by saying "car." A word spoken in response conveys that the adult heard, understood, and accepted the child's utterance as valid. This encourages the child to say more. Word responses also help the child broaden his vocabulary and ideas.

Vocalizations

Pre-speech vocalizations can be entertaining and intriguing for a child, drawing him into dialogue when words fail. Your vocalizations can let the child know you heard him and you accept his utterance as an initiation in a dialogue. In the Jessica Dialogue, her mother says, "Ooooo" and Jessica makes raspberry sounds in response. Apraxic children who do not respond to speech often respond quite well to sounds. Therefore, sounds can be a powerful tool for drawing an inattentive child to dialogue and speech.

Actions

Excessive gestures, facial expressions, and other actions can be used to draw a child into communication and dialogue when sounds and words are ineffective. Actions can be used as response turns in dialogue. These actions include hand and arm gestures, body movements, facial expressions, or the interaction of dolls and toys. For example, a toy dog might hop up and down and "bark" every time the child makes a sound. Because actions are perceived visually, apraxic children often find them easier to attend to than spoken words.

Imitations of the Child

One of the most powerful tools in developing dialogue is to respond to the child's spontaneous utterance by imitating him. Thus, instead of expecting the child to imitate us, we model how to take turns by imitating him. In the Jessica Dialogue, the mother imitates the child by making a raspberry sound after the child does. When an adult repeats it back to the child, it teaches the child how to match sounds and shows him that people can say the same thing in turn with one another.

Give the Child a Silent Pause

Do your know the term *pregnant pause*? It's the silent point in dialogue when the party who has just spoken becomes quiet and waits for the other party to speak. A silent pause is what gives a turn back to the child. In the Jessica Dialogue, the mother pauses frequently to give the turn back to the child. The pause is pregnant with the anticipation of the child's comment—it begs a response by the other party. The pregnant pause is a profound tool in the development of imitation skill. Silence communicates to the child that it is his turn to speak.

If an adult does not pause to give a baby or a young child a chance to speak, then the potential dialogue and imitation skills could be diminished. The following case of Tyler, who was not apraxic, but dysarthric, illustrates such a problem.

Tyler

Tyler was four years of age, had a severe neuromuscular disorder, and was described by his parents as being nonverbal. The parents asked me if I thought he would talk someday. Within the first ten minutes of our session, I heard Tyler say at least twenty spontaneous but unclear words. I asked the parents to help me make a list of all the words they had heard him say. At the end of our session, we had over 150 words on that list! Some of these words had been heard numerous times, like "no" and "Mom." Others had been heard perhaps only once.

Tyler's speech was very distorted due to the motor disability, but even with severe dysarthria and subsequent unintelligibility it was quite clear that he was saying a huge number of words. Why would these bright parents even consider him nonverbal?

Over the next few months, I discovered the reason. They did all the talking and paused infrequently for him to speak. For example, one day Tyler's mother tried to get him to say "blue." She said, "Tyler, what color is the car? Do you see the car? See the car. It's a nice little car. You like cars. You like cars a lot. You have lots of cars at home. What color is the car, Tyler? What color is it? You know what color it is. Can you see it? You know your colors. You know green and pink and red. You know what color it is. See the car?"

Finally, she paused, but Tyler did not say a word. What could he say? What question was he answering? Even though his mother finally gave him a turn to talk, his mind was moving and he said nothing. So she began again, rambling on about colors, cars, and how smart Tyler was. She never gave him a chance to respond to the initial question: What color is the car?

Tyler was enrolled in two one-hour sessions of speech and language therapy per week. I began the imitation process with him by responding directly to the words he said as if they were initiation turns. I offered silent pauses immediately following my response. I did not teach him any new words, because he already had plenty. And I did not work on any specific consonant or vowel sounds. I simply responded to his spontaneous utterances with a word or two and then I paused.

Within two months, Tyler and I were exchanging long dialogue sequences together and he was aware that I was listening to his every word. He began to speak more slowly and carefully, so that I could understand more of what he said. For his turns, he also began repeating words. When I could not understand the prior turn, he repeated them with more force and watched me carefully as I repeated back to him what he said. At the end of four months, and with some training for them, Tyler's parents also began to hear, listen to, and respond to his spontaneous word productions. They began to understand more of what he said because they were listening harder and because Tyler had learned to speak more clearly.

For Tyler, the rewards of pausing had an immediate and profound effect: He began to talk more often, he began to speak up and enunciate better, and he began to try to say a greater variety of vowels and consonants. This child already could imitate words, obviously, but he had no one with whom to dialogue in turn. Without his communication partners pausing to give him a turn he had not learned any strategies for improving his speech.

Including Pauses in Therapy

Pausing during therapy can be a difficult discipline for some therapists, teachers, and parents. Do not be afraid or uncomfortable with frequent and long pauses. Remember, it helps give the turn back to the child and encourages him to say more. A dialogue early in therapy might look something like the following.

Truck Dialogue

CHILD	THERAPIST
Truck.	Truck. Right. [Pause]
[No turn]	[Continued pausing]
Truck.	That' s a truck! [Pause]
[No turn]	[Continued pausing]
[No turn]	[Continued pausing]
Roommm!	Roommm!
Roommm!	Roommm! [Pause]
[No turn]	[Pause]
[Reaches for a truck]	There' s another truck. A big truck. [Hands him a truck]
Big truck.	Truck . . . truck . . . truck.
[Takes truck]	[Pause]
[No turn]	[Continued pausing]
[No turn]	[Continued pausing]
Big truck.	Another big truck!

A dialogue like this can be slow and almost painful! A child at this level of imitation development may say only five to ten things in 30 minutes. It can seem at times as if you are doing nothing. For parents, teachers, and therapists who are anxious for the nonverbal apraxic child to begin talking, doing nothing seems wrong, but it is exactly what many of these children need. The silence you give to the child allows him to process the dialogue. It allows him a moment to play with the toy (a reward for speaking). It allows you to hear the next spontaneous utterance. All of these things help build the dialogue framework.

I monitor progress at this level of imitation training in several ways. For example, in the initial therapy session, I will count the number of utterances the child makes during that time and then compare that to the number he makes during the same activity weeks or months later. Dialogue factors that show positive change include:

1. Decreased number of pauses
2. Decreased length of individual pauses
3. Increased number of utterances in a unit of time
4. Improved orientation to the sounds and words you say
5. Increased number of contexts in which key utterances are spoken

Apraxic children who respond positively to this type of therapy usually do so within the first three months of treatment. If there are changes to the above five measures by the end of three months, then you can be sure therapy is having a positive effect on the child's dialogue abilities and further therapy is warranted.

If no changes are seen in these five areas, seriously reconsider the approach you are taking in treatment. Try another three months of similar therapy, for a total of six months—especially if the child is very young. If no changes are noted by the end of six months, an augmentative method of communication will be needed for a much longer time. When I see no change in the above five parameters after six months, I usually recommend that we back off from these methods and try them at a later date.

Don't be afraid to introduce these techniques to older children or conduct routine probes of their abilities. I have seen several nonverbal, severely apraxic clients respond positively to these methods as teenagers and young adults. Although the methods may need to be shelved for a while, parents and therapists should be aware that these skills can emerge much later.

Allow the Child to Say Anything

Once the apraxic child's initiation is responded to, and once the turn has been given back to him via a silent pause, the child now has an opportunity to say something more. If the child speaks for this turn, the important thing to realize is that this second utterance will be a spontaneous and self-generated sound unrelated to those made previously by the adult or the child. It simply will be whatever the child feels like saying at that moment. This is why I call each part of the exchange a one-step dialogue: Each child initiation and adult response is composed of only one step.

This process is seen clearly in the Truck Dialogue above. Each comment the child makes is an original and spontaneous utterance that has no real relationship to prior utterances or to the response turn of the adult. The topic is on trucks because the child and therapist are playing with trucks, but each remark the child makes is an original word. The therapist treats each of the child's utterances as initiations and tries to create a dialogue frame. However, the long periods of silence from the child indicates he does not grasp the therapist's parameters of dialogue. The child therefore must be allowed to say whatever he wants for his next turn.

In the Jessica Dialogue, notice the relationship between what the mother says and what the child says. Most of the time, the baby says something unique for her turns. When the mother says "Hi sweetie, are you a good baby?" the child responds by saying "Oooo." When the mother says "Oooo," the child smiles. The important thing here is that the child takes a turn, not that she says or does what her communication partner says or does.

Anyone who has interacted with a baby or a severely apraxic child at this level of imitation and conversational skill development knows that they cannot force them to say what they want them to say. Instead of fighting against the apraxic child's drive to initiate, allow the child to lead the dialogue and to say whatever he wants for his turns. When we allow the child to lead the dialogue and when we respond to him, we build the dialogue frame and encourage the child to say more.

Chapter Seven

Mutual Imitation: The Most Important Stage

Once dialogue routines begin to appear, a baby moves to the next stage of imitation development, where more mature imitation can be observed. Jean Piaget called it *mutual imitation*. In infancy, mutual imitation means that children can imitate themselves if we imitate them while they are already engaged in making a target sound. This is where we hear the child say the same sound purposefully in sequence. At this stage, babies gain significant skill in discriminating the similarities between:

- The auditory features of the sounds they produce (what they hear)
- The tactile sensations of the sounds they produce (what they feel in the mouth, nose, face and throat)
- The proprioceptive features of the sounds they produce (what they sense about their jaw, lip, and tongue movements)

Auditory, tactile and proprioceptive experiences comprise the internal image of every sound a baby makes. They use this combined image to remember and recreate sounds in vocal play.

The Baby Jack Dialogue is typical of this stage of imitation development.

Baby Jack Dialogue

Baby Jack	Mommy Jill
Oooo.	Hi sweetie.
Oooo.	Oooo.
Oooo.	Oooo.
Gggggg.	Oooo.
[Squeak.]	[Laugh.] Hi. Hi, Jack.
Oooo.	Oooo.
Oooo.	Oooo.

Notice that Jack begins the exchange and Mommy continues to respond—the back-and-forth dialogue routine. These are skills he learned in the previous stage. Also, notice the new features that mark this dialogue as more advanced:

1. Jack says the same sound multiple times.
2. When Mommy Jill imitates the baby for her turn, it appears that Baby Jack is imitating her for his turn.
3. When Mommy Jill says something original Jack does not imitate her.

Although it appears that the child is imitating the adult, he is not. He is imitating *himself* within the frame. The baby has gained enough sound control to repeat it several times in a row. This gives the child an opportunity to compare his own sounds with the adult's as turns are taken.

Have you ever tried to show off a baby's speech skills when he is at this stage of development? A parent might say, "He can say 'Oooo.' Watch." The adventurous parent then spends the next five minutes trying to show off how the child can say "Oooo," but the child never does because he does not have the ability to imitate *you*. He only has the ability to imitate *himself*. Therefore, he can perform his sounds and use them in sequence only if you catch him while he is engaged in the sound.

Mutual Imitation and Childhood Apraxia

Minimally verbal apraxic children have not reached this level of imitation skill and cannot repeat sounds or words in sequence within a dialogue frame. They also are unable to do so at the request of another within the frame. As a result, the apraxic child is unable to imitate new sounds or words from models presented within that dialogue.

Since apraxic children are unable to constructively participate in dialogue, each utterance tends to be original, spontaneous, and cannot be drawn out. These children cannot imitate another person's words on demand. In the most severe cases, these children produce a random assortment of sounds or words that cannot be elicited at all.

Watch this carefully and don't be fooled into thinking that the child who does participate in dialogue is able to imitate mutually. The key question is: Who is leading the conversation? Many of these children can carry on conversations as long as they are in the initiator role, but they cannot or will not participate if put into the responder role. When we respond to their utterances, we create one-step dialogues, not true dialogues.

Rules for Using Mutual Imitation

To treat the delay of expressive speech and language with apraxic children, we can create dialogues by responding to their utterances. The child can say the same sound many times in sequence within the new dialogue frame.

Similar to the previous aspects of imitation training, mutual imitation routines require a change in the way adults work. The following is a set of rules for engaging in mutual imitation that will help your child's skills bloom.

Put Primary Emphasis on Imitating the Child

Listen carefully to the sounds your child makes and imitate them for your turn. This is the key to mutual imitation. We want the child to say the sound he just said again and again and again. Each time he says a particular sound, we should imitate it no matter how many times we say the sound in sequence. If we spend twenty minutes saying the same sound or word over and over again, good! We want him to become consistent in making sounds and words, and we want him to take control of those sounds.

New sounds and words can be modeled at this time, but do not expect your child to imitate them. Most likely, he will not be ready, although he is getting closer. Focus on the sequences of sounds throughout the dialogue.

Celebrate Mature Imitation When It Happens

If your child imitates a new sound or word on occasion during this process, celebrate! But do not be fooled into believing that he is ready to move on to the next level of imitation. Most children, both "normal" children and those with childhood apraxia, will begin to imitate novel or new sounds and words during this time. New sounds and words just show up or pop out on occasion, but they don't stick around. So, don't stop engaging in mutual imitation. Your child will be better off in the long run if you stick solidly to this level of imitation for some time.

Don't Worry About His Ability to Answer Questions Yet

Asking questions of your child puts him in the responder role. At this stage of imitation, your child should still be in the initiator role while you take the responder role. Feel free to ask him questions to stimulate this next level of language development, but do not expect him to answer with words. For example, when asked, "Where are your shoes?" your child probably will run off and get his shoes instead of answer your question. When asked, "Do you want some juice?" he'll go to the refrigerator, hold up his glass, or go sit at the table instead of saying "Yes." When asked, "What's your name?" or "How old are you?" your child probably will respond with silence.

If your child spontaneously says a word, you can respond with a question. For example, if the child wants juice and says "juice," feel free to respond with something like, "Do you want juice?" The child will probably respond with silence if he does not yet take that next turn, but you never know when the ability to mutually imitate may appear. Without expecting it, the child may answer by saying "juice." Do not be fooled into thinking that the child answered the question. He only has repeated himself within the turn sequence. He is imitating mutually and, while this is wonderful, it is the not really the ability to answer the question.

Imitate the Child Multiple Times per Day

Engage in this form of imitation many times per day. For example, imitate your child as you dress him, feed him, bathe him, drive to the store with him, swing him, dance with him, build a Lego structure with him, and tuck him into bed. Any time of day or night can be a time to imitate your child. The best times are when you are not distracted by other things or interrupted by other people. You want to engage in concentrated periods of mutual imitation every day.

Imitate the Child for Several Turns per Engagement

Each time you imitate your child, pass the turn back to him to give a back-and-forth nature to the dialogue. Other people who say things and imitate the turns will disengage this process, so again, try to do it during one-on-one time.

Slowly Increase Turns within the Mutual-Imitation Dialogue

One of the best techniques you have for helping your apraxic child move from this stage to the next one is to increase the number of turns that you and the child take in the dialogue. The longer the exchange carries on, the more difficult it will become to determine who is leading and who is following in the turns. When that line becomes blurred, the next stage emerges.

Teach Others to Hear and Imitate the Child

You will want to ensure that all the people who have regular contact with your apraxic child are listening carefully and are able to discriminate what he is already saying. This may require you to point out specific sounds the child is making. You might say, "Can you hear him? Mmmah. Mmmah. He's saying Mommy."

Once others become aware of the sounds your child makes, teach them to imitate him while they interact with him. Say, for example, "When he says 'beeee' say that right after him. Try to sound just like him. He will like it and he may say it again. We want him to practice his sounds as much as possible."

Play with Sound for the Sake of Play

It is important to keep your child focused on sound. Reread chapter 2 for ideas and examples of ways to play with sound, and use these as opportunities to play with mutual-imitation sequences.

Treat Utterances as Having Meaning and Purpose

You can and should treat many of these utterances as meaningful. For example, respond to your child by saying, "Mmmah! Ma. Mamma. You said, 'Mama.'"

Build in Quiet Times

Do not engage in mutual imitation all the time with your child. If you do, you will teach your child to expect you to respond to him whenever he pleases. You do not want to give him that much power and control over you. Our apraxic children, just like all children, need to learn how to interact with us and they need to learn to be quiet!

Quiet times should be considered a part of this program from the beginning. Tell your child, for example, "I'm busy right now. I can't talk. We can talk later." And then ignore him if he persists. If he disobeys, use your basic behavior management strategies.

Provide a Large Wall Mirror for Play

A mirror can become a child's best toy during the stage of mutual imitation. A large wall mirror in which the child can watch himself produce sound can be a focal point for learning to rehearse sounds as well as to practice facial expressions and other arm, hand, and leg gestures. Place a large floor-length mirror on the wall in your child's room, in the bathroom, in the hall, or anywhere else that is convenient. Consider hanging a wall mirror so that it reaches down to the wall baseboard. Then your child can see himself from head to toe.

WARNING: Do not let a young child play with a glass mirror that is not attached to a wall or door. Plexiglas mirrors are better for that.

Moving On

The stage of mutual imitation is the primary one to help children develop their ability to hear and recognize the similarities and differences between sounds and words. During this stage, children gain mastery over their own productions. They begin to say occasional words during this period, but their new ability to do so does not signal that they now have mastery over speech.

Once mutual imitation becomes a regular part of your interactions with the apraxic child, you are ready to move on to the next stage. But be warned! Many children at this level appear ready but still need considerable time to learn how to recognize and control production over the great variations of sound possible in our language. Therefore, it is strongly recommended that you continue to work at this level for some time.

Chapter Eight

Imitating the Repertoire: A Significant
Breakthrough for Imitation Skill

Children who are aware of sound, play with sound, engage in dialogue using sound, and are becoming proficient at making the same sound multiple times in sequence are at the threshold of the breakthrough stage of imitation. Piaget called it *spontaneous imitation of old repertoire.*

A child's repertoire is the set of vocalizations he has learned to say regularly and consistently. These are the sounds he is aware of and learning to master. We'll refer to them as "his sounds." At this point, a baby's sound repertoire has been developing for eight to ten months. Whether the child is vocal or somewhat quiet, these are the sounds that are heard and with which he is learning to imitate. His repertoire will include at least:

- Coos and goos
- A variety of raspberries
- Giggles, chuckles, and laughs
- Grunts and growls
- Sniffs, snorts, pants, and whispers
- Squeals, yells, and shouts
- Rising and falling stresses and intonation patterns
- An expanding repertoire of vowels
- An emerging small set of consonants
- An emerging set of consonant and vowel sequences

71

The "emerging set of consonant and vowel sequences" is usually called by the more familiar term *babbling*. Children babble when they string consonants and vowels together into sequences like, "ba-ba-ba-ba," and, "do-do-do-do." This is the child's playful and rhythmic experimentation with these sounds. When they babble, infants usually use the voiced stops (*b, d, g*), the voiced nasals (*m, n, ng*), and the voiced glides (*w, l, y*) along with several vowels. From this point forward, the child will engage in vocal play and dialogues using babbling sequences like these and the other vocalizations listed above.

What makes this stage of imitation unique is that now an adult can encourage a baby to say these sounds. Let's take a look at a sample dialogue that shows this level of imitation at work.

Old Repertoire Dialogue

Child	Parent
	Say "baba" for grandma. Baba.
[Silence]	Baba. Baba.
[Silence]	Baba. Baba.
Baba.	That' s it! Baba!
Baba.	Baba!

There are two outstanding new features of dialogue at this breakthrough stage. First, the adult is able to be the initiator who models the sound to be imitated. Second, the baby has assumed the responder role because he now has enough capacity, consistency, and control to follow the adult's lead. This is a huge milestone in the evolution of imitation skill for an individual child. For the first time in his life, the baby can respond to what the adult is initiating. As stated above, the target sound modeled by the adult must be one the child has previously rehearsed.

It is important to realize that although a baby is able to imitate his sounds, he will not take a turn and imitate every time. Notice in the Old Repertoire Dialogue that, at first, the baby did not respond to the adult model. Anyone who has ever tried to get a baby or a young child to perform on demand will recognize this phenomenon. Here, we are not concerned about a child's willingness to imitate on demand. We are concerned about his *capacity* to do so. In this stage, babies develop the capacity to imitate old repertoire sounds on demand, but they may not perform them if they are in a foul mood or are distracted. Regardless of willingness, the ability to imitate his own repertoire of sounds on demand is within the child's ability range.

The ability to imitate rehearsed vocalizations precedes his ability to imitate new sounds. With "old sounds," a baby learns to make an identical response turn within a dialogue frame without the added burden of trying to make a new sound. He uses old sounds to learn how to become proficient in the act of imitating, so he can use that skill to learn new sounds later.

Children with Apraxia

Children with apraxia may or may not have reached this level of imitation skill. Some of these children have the capacity to imitate their old repertoire sounds; others do not. Some can produce their own sounds inconsistently; others can imitate a few of their sounds this way. Most have too few sounds and too little practice with them to use them efficiently in old repertoire dialogue exchanges. Some severely apraxic children produce only a specific small set of sounds or words with limited control and flexibility in dialogue frames. All of these problems result in the apraxic child's inability to manipulate sound and to play with sound as a differential skill in conversation with others.

An adult's reaction to a child's lack of skill can compound the problem. Often, family members, teachers, and therapists just ignore the few pre-speech vocalizations and unintelligible words that the apraxic child produces. Thus, the child loses the opportunity to learn how to imitate with the very sounds and words he can say.

In some cases, so much focus is directed to a child's augmentative communication system that his spontaneous vocalizations are ignored completely. The case of Danielle in chapter 6 is a perfect illustration. The only real speech-like utterance Danielle made was "adah." That sound was ignored by everyone around her while she was being taught to communicate with signs and gestures. As her parents explained to me in our first meeting, "We used to think she was saying 'daddy,' but she says it all the time whether or not daddy is around. So we've just been ignoring it."

Without an understanding of the stages of imitation development, there was no way for Danielle's parents to understand the value of this sound. When they tried to get her to say other words like "momma" or "juice," she was silent. The decision to teach her to use basic sign language was a logical one because it appeared that it would be a long time before she might ever talk.

As I began to work with Danielle, however, and as others continued her sign language training, I began to pay very close attention to this sound and to respond to it as if she had said it with a purpose. Within a few months, Danielle and I were saying "adah" back and forth in dialogue turns and imitating each other by changing the prosodic features of the utterance—length, pitch, intonation, loudness, syllable stress—and by altering its vowels.

Over the next year, Danielle learned how to dialogue and to imitate at various levels using this same sound. First, she learned to use it to initiate dialogue as I responded to it every time she uttered it. Second, she engaged in mutual imitation turns as I imitated the sound perfectly after she uttered it. Third, she engaged in spontaneous imitation of old repertoire as she imitated the sound after my model. Finally, she began to alter it in turn with me.

My focus of treatment shifted from saying new things to helping her imitate sounds she already knew. I used the same sound for about one year. After she learned what imitation was, and as new sounds emerged through other respiratory, phonatory, and oral-motor means, Danielle began to imitate an increasingly bigger repertoire of both pre-speech and speech sounds. Throughout this process, Danielle's augmentative communication methods—including both sign language and computer work—continued and became increasingly complex. After nearly two years, Danielle began to imitate all kinds of new sounds and words and engage in simple verbal dialogues. Here's a sample from one of our final days together:

DANIELLE	PAM
Adah?	What' s that? That' s a garbage truck.
Uck.	Yes, truck.
Uck.	Truck.
[Silence.]	Do you see the other truck?
Uck?	The other truck.
Uh-uh uck.	Yes, other truck. Where' s the other truck?
Uck. [Picks out other truck.]	There it is.
Sss.	Sss. There it isss.
Sss.	Truck.
Uck.	Can you find the boat?
Oat.	Boat. Where' s the boat?
Oat.	Do you have a boat?
Es (yes).	

This is a beautiful dialogue for a severely involved apraxic child who is just beginning to imitate spontaneously from her expanding old repertoire of sounds. It is a dialogue that will continue to become more complex with time. With the ability to imitate any old repertoire sound comes the ability to attempt many words. For example, as "ee" emerged, Danielle could use it to say any word in which long *e* was a main vowel, including single-syllable words like *three, pee, me, see,* and *whee*; and multiple-syllable words like *Christmas tree, Bambi, Sneezy,* and *Grumpy.*

Do you see how speech and imitation development in normal babies runs counter to much of what we do to stimulate speech and language expression in severely apraxic children? In typical treatment, we present new sounds for the child to imitate with the expectation that he has the ability to imitate and that he will do so when he figures out how to make the sounds involved. We usually attribute his lack of speech to a lack of sound. But the apraxic child's inability to develop vocal speech is a failure in two areas. First, the apraxic child does *not* know how to say the sounds, and second he does *not* know how to imitate speech.

With the ability to produce old repertoire sounds on demand comes the ability to speak with others. This is tremendous encouragement for producing verbal language. I have seen its positive impact on countless children with severe childhood apraxia. Once they can imitate their own sounds spontaneously in dialogues with one other person, they begin to develop their sound-making skill rapidly and become highly motivated to communicate. The shear number of utterances they make in one unit of time increases dramatically. The more time spent trying to repeat specific old repertoire sounds, the greater the child's skill. Confidence improves and risk-taking increases as he becomes more flexible in saying these sounds.

There are two other important factors about spontaneous imitation of old repertoire. First, it's fun! Making familiar and easy sounds elevates therapy from the serious to the sensational. Kids who avoid being taught find this work a relief from the rest of the teaching they might be experiencing. It's easy, it's different, and it's engaging.

Second, it's satisfying. To take turns back and forth with another person gratifies one's deepest need to communicate. The child discovers that someone is listening to him. A therapist who devotes one full hour of weekly therapy to listening to and responding to every utterance the child makes, and who does her best to get the child to say these things again and again, soon finds herself on top of the child's list of best friends. The motiva-

76

tion to engage in this practice strikes a deep chord, and a severely apraxic child begins to anticipate each subsequent session with mounting enthusiasm.

Finally, the number of communication partners for the apraxic child increases dramatically as parents, siblings, teachers, friends, and therapists integrate turn-taking into their communication routines with him. The child finds that he can participate freely, even while hampered by vocal, phonological, and articulation restrictions.

Using Old Repertoire Sounds to Stimulate Imitation

Severely apraxic children need to develop the ability to imitate a core set of old repertoire vocalizations. It's a powerful tool in facilitating verbal speech. The following suggestions will help you begin the process.

Create the Dialogue Frame

Get the dialogue going with mutual imitation routines, as described in previous chapters. Begin to insert spontaneous imitation of old repertoire sounds within those frames.

Take the Initiator Role

Take the initiator role in the dialogue by modeling the child's sounds. Watch to see if the child imitates you during his turn. If he does, you can be sure he has begun to move into the stage of spontaneous imitation of old repertoire. If he doesn't, try again periodically until he shows evidence of this skill.

Expect the Responder Role

Your child should begin to imitate old repertoire sounds when they are presented within dialogue frames. He will do it once in a while, but not all the time.

Know the Child's Repertoire

Become very familiar with the sounds your child makes. Use these for your modeled utterances. And keep a list of the spontaneous sounds your child produces. It's a handy tool that can be expanded as new sounds are added. Each time the child utters a sound, he is telling you, "This is one of my sounds."

Model Sounds Precisely

Don't model "Oooo" if the child actually says "awww." Make sure you model sounds with the same intonation, pitch, loudness, and vowel and consonant patterns your child uses. In many cases, this will feel like you are learning a new language. In a way, you are. You're learning the child's own personal language. Go there to communicate with him, and then gradually bring his productions in line with yours.

Praise Imitations

Your child's newfound ability to imitate sound on demand should be celebrated. It's a breakthrough in his training!

Broaden the Audience

Build an increasingly wider range of people with whom your child will use this new skill. Remember, he may perform for you but for no one else at first. Add a new person to this circle one-at-a-time until he is able to do this with almost anyone. Do not make a circus act of this skill, of course, but try to broaden his audience in a natural way appropriate to your personalities.

Expect Errors

Remember, this is still a rehearsal of sounds—play at a new level of imitative ability. Be delighted even if it is not what you would call speech.

Celebrate the Small Set

Don't worry if your child can say only a few different sounds, and don't worry if he still has no words. Remember Danielle? She used "adah" for about a year as she learned to imitate. Your child is learning to imitate with his old repertoire of sounds. Therefore, he may not imitate any new sounds or words for a while. Don't fret. Teach him the process of imitation now and he will learn to imitate new sounds and words later.

Wait for the Mood

When babies are at this stage of imitation development, they do not always imitate on demand. They imitate when they are in the mood and when their attention is focused on sound and on you. Catch your child in this position and rehearse imitation with him at that time. Do not force imitation on him too often or when he is not in the mood; he will tune you out. Try to include imitation practice within the natural ebb and flow of dialogue with your child, and sprinkle it into your interactions with him throughout the day.

Describe the Process to the Child

We don't tell babies that we are teaching them to imitate, because they wouldn't understand. But it often helps to explain what we are doing to older apraxic children. Say, for example, "You said it, and I said it. We're saying the same thing." Show delight in this.

Create Routines

Watch carefully for routine ways you can encourage your child to rehearse his sounds on demand. For example, if he has begun to growl, have your child imitate his growl after you by pretending it's a motor sound every time you head for the car. Remember to use only old repertoire sounds at this level.

Devise Games

Use the child's old repertoire sounds as part of a simple game. For example, help your child make a block structure and hold some of the blocks in your lap. Then ask him to say one of his sounds each time he wants another one. Receiving the block becomes the reward for saying one of his sounds.

Assign Meaning to Consistent Vocalizations

As your child becomes proficient at saying his own sounds on demand, give certain ones a meaning that will be shared between the two of you and others. For example, if the child can say "mmm," have him say it when you give him food.

Equate His Productions with Real Words

Model real words and then model your child's old repertoire production for him to imitate. For example, say, "That boy's name is Isaac. Isaac. Say, 'I'." Expect your child to imitate his sound and then reward him for saying the word. Exclaim, "You said, 'Isaac'!"

Rehearse with Ease

Get the child to rehearse his sounds without realizing how hard he is working. It is much more important that the child rehearse his old repertoire sounds than learn new ones. He will learn new sounds in the next level. For now, focus on drilling familiar sounds.

Note All New Sounds

Recognize that new sounds will emerge regularly throughout this stage. Add these new sounds to the set of sounds you stimulate on a regular basis.

Allow for Child Preference

Children usually show a preference for new sounds at the expense of old ones. Don't worry about it. Drop the old sounds for a while and let the child assimilate the new ones. Reintroduce the old ones after the new sounds lose their novelty. Some sounds will make a strong appearance for a while and then disappear for months at a time, only to reappear unexpectedly later.

Expect Words to Appear

As the child gains more vocal control, and as he begins to use sound meaningfully in dialogues, many of his utterances will become real words. Expect it, but do not count on it. Your child's imitation skill is flourishing but not fully formed. New words should be treated just like new sounds: Model them for him to imitate. Even though new sounds and words are making their appearance, your child still needs work on the ability to recognize the similarities and differences between sounds and words and will continue to learn about this while engaged in mutual imitation and spontaneous imitation within repertoire.

Respect the Child's Phonetic Acquisition Patterns

Children with severe apraxia usually blaze their own trail through the forest of phoneme acquisition. Don't expect yours to follow the "normal" path. Listen carefully for the child's own personal set of emerging phonemes and focus on those. It is common for a severely apraxic child to acquire difficult-to-produce sounds like "r" or "l" before easy-to-produce ones like "g" or "n." Do not ignore those sounds that are coming along just because they shouldn't be there yet.

Honor the Child's Idiosyncratic Phonological Patterns

Severely apraxic children acquire their own phonological patterns that may not be like the average. For example, one child with whom I worked for several years gained every phoneme in isolation and used them as real words before ever stringing simple vowels and consonants together in simple one-syllable words. To compound this, she produced words by uttering the final sound of the word she attempted. She said "ee" for *Bambi* and "n" for *Christopher Robin*. I had to recognize each sound she spoke as a real word for her and then engage in dialogues of single sounds as if they were dialogues of real words.

To her parents and teachers, this child had not begun to talk. But actually, she was saying literally hundreds of words by uttering the final sound of each word. We must analyze, understand, and honor these idiosyncratic phonological patterns if we are to make headway at the level of spontaneous imitation of old repertoire.

Chapter Nine

New Sounds and Words: Reaching
Success in the Final Stage

This is the final stage of imitation development, the stage Jean Piaget termed *spontaneous imitation of new repertoire*. So far, the child has learned to enjoy making sound, to participate in dialogue routines with sound, to repeat his own sounds in vocal play and in dialogue with others, and to imitate another person who models vocalizations he knows. These experiences have drawn the child's attention to his own sound-making activities and have helped him to attend to the speech of others. As a result, he can discriminate similarities and differences in vocal productions and produce specific sounds at will. In short, he has gone through a developmental process that has taught him how to imitate pre-speech vocalizations.

In this final stage, the child reaches maturity in imitation development and learns to say specific sounds in specific arrangements for specific words—his first words. Most adults think that a child's first words mark the beginning of imitation skill. But as we have seen, the imitation of words marks the end of a long process. At about one year of age, the baby coordinates all of his previously learned skills and speaks adult words. He begins to sequence sounds in new ways and build a new repertoire.

For example, during the pre-speech stage, a particular child may have learned to say many different sounds, including consonant *b* and vowel *i*. He will have spent countless hours rehearsing them in the context of vocal play and primitive dialogues with others. In this final stage, parents can model a novel way to combine both of these sounds into a word such as *bye-bye*. A parent can say to the child, "Say, 'bye-bye'," and expect the child to say something close to the mark. The parent is helping the child to leap from meaningless babble to meaningful words. If the child truly has entered this final stage, he will be able to do it.

How many times have we witnessed a parent trying to get their baby to say a word like *bye-bye*? They model the word countless times. They take the baby's arm and flap it into a waving motion. They ask the baby to say it. We hear them say, "Come on. You can say it. Bye-bye. Bye-bye. Come on, sweet. Bye-bye. Tell grandma 'bye-bye'." Still, the baby will not say the word until he is ready, and part of what makes him ready is his ability to imitate. The baby speaks when all the underlying skills of imitation development converge.

As was described in chapter 1, a child's first words usually are anticipated with passion and, when they arrive, are greeted with great joy. But like learning to ride a bike, the toddler's ability to imitate new words is a little shaky at first. He needs some time to solidify the skill. Readers who have witnessed the emergence of first words in babies and toddlers can testify that these early words come and go with irritating irregularity. Once a child can say "bye-bye," there is no guarantee that he will say it on demand.

Underlying this is a developmental pattern that governs how and when a young child will imitate words on demand. This pattern mirrors the same stages of imitation development that the child just completed with sound. That is, children seem to go through the same stages of imitation development in word productions that they do with sound productions. This time, however, they go through the levels much quicker—in weeks or months instead of a full year. The levels are as follows:

- LEVEL 1: The child says his new words occasionally, spontaneously, and unconsciously, but cannot say them on demand or after a model (vocal contagion).

- LEVEL 2: The child's spontaneous words are used in turn in dialogue frames created by others (dialogue).
- LEVEL 3: The child repeats his word multiple times within the dialogue frame (mutual imitation).
- LEVEL 4: The child says his words in imitation of others (spontaneous imitation of old repertoire).
- LEVEL 5: The child repeats any new word as a response turn in imitation of others (spontaneous imitation of new repertoire).

Jean Piaget did not report these levels in the normal children he observed, but I have noted this developmental process in countless hundreds of children with apraxia. Piaget did not see these levels for two reasons. First, he was not looking for them. Once his children began to imitate words, he thought the process was complete. Second, because normal children go through this process so quickly, they are difficult to detect.

Apraxic children go through these levels very slowly, often spending months at each one. Thus, documenting each level is easier. After observing these levels in apraxic children, it is easier to see them in toddlers.

Level 1—Vocal Contagion

The child says his new words occasionally, spontaneously, and unconsciously, but cannot say them on demand or after a model.

A toddler's first words seem to pop out unexpectedly and without planning or prodding. For example, the child may be playing with a doll and suddenly say "baby." Once spoken, however, the child may appear completely unaware that he has said the word. Have you seen a baby say his first word and the adults around him go crazy with excitement? Then you probably noticed that the child had no idea what was going on. And when the adults tried to get the child to say the word again, he didn't.

When first words emerge, a child has no real control over what he is saying. It's a natural phenomena that arises almost without him knowing it. Just like spontaneously reaching for a toy on a shelf, the child's first word just comes out. And because the act is virtually unconscious, it is almost impossible to get the child to say the word again. Imagine asking a baby to "reach for that toy the same way you just did." A baby does not know what he did; therefore, he has no capacity to do it again. The child may laugh, smile, clap, and be generally adorable in response to your enthusiastic prodding, but he will not reach for that toy nor say that word again. Not right away, at least.

At this stage of early word emergence, parents will never know when their child will produce a word. They simply must wait and listen for the word to appear suddenly. These are *pop-out words*. In my experience, pop-out words dominate the expressive speech of typical developing toddlers throughout the acquisition of their first twenty words or so. During this time, parents usually have a terrible time showing off the child's skill to others. They want so desperately to share this thrill, but usually they are disappointed in the attempt.

Pop-Out Words and Apraxic Children

One of the primary characteristics of the severely apraxic child who has begun to say words is that all of his words pop out spontaneously. It is almost impossible to get him to produce the words voluntarily. For example, he may be able to say "momma" easily when he wants his mother, but he is completely unable to say "momma" when asked to say it. Parents report this to me all the time. "He says 'momma' once in a while, but he can't talk." What they mean is that the word *momma* pops out occasionally, but they cannot get him to say it when they want him to, and they can't get him to say other words on demand either.

Parents also report that their apraxic children used to say certain words, as in, "He used to say 'dadda', but he doesn't anymore." For a short period of time, a certain word popped out just enough that the family noticed it. But because the child gained no voluntary control over the word, he stopped using it. When the parents tried to get him to say the word, they were met with silence and began to think the word was lost. The most common of these reported pop-out words are *momma*, *dada*, and *no*, but any word might be used. One parent told me that the child had said "turkey" several times on Thanksgiving and then never said it again.

It is my experience that pop-out words dominate the expressive speech of severely apraxic children well past their first words. The process can persist as expressive language moves into long utterances. Even apraxic children who are functioning with three-to-five-word utterances can still be relying on spontaneous declarations without the ability to imitate specific words or sounds on demand. This is the "motor planning" problem of the apraxic child: the ability to know how to say a sound or word spontaneously without the ability to say it consciously or voluntarily. Generally, this is viewed as a movement problem, but it also can be a stage-of-imitation problem. It's more in the intellectual or cognitive arena than in the muscle or motor arena.

When pop-out words dominate, adults can become frustrated when trying to get their apraxic child to say a particular word or sound on demand. For example, when a child has been heard to say "juice" once in a while, we begin to expect him to say it whenever he wants juice. But the apraxic child needs time to solidify this skill. Often, he doesn't understand that he is supposed to say his word *now*. Frustration comes when we think, *He could say it if only he tried.* True, but he does not know how to try.

An apraxic child who is verbal but stuck in this level of imitation development will dominate conversations. Real dialogue only exists with him when we respond to his spontaneous pop-out words. When we turn the tables and ask him to respond to things we've said, or to imitate novel sounds or words we've presented, the child shows us in multiple ways that he cannot. He switches topics, ignores us, or merrily goes along saying whatever he wants to say. We usually attribute these behaviors to personality quirks or simple stubbornness, but I see this as an imitation-maturation delay.

These children cannot participate in dialogue because they do not attend to our initiation turns and take response turns in nice dialogue sequences. As such, they are unable to play with words in dialogue the way a typical developing baby or toddler can. Thus, they lack the sound-and-word-matching experiences that teach them how to alter their utterances purposefully.

When the child is saying words spontaneously but not in imitation turns, the best approach is to set up situations in which the child is most likely to say words—any words. For example, if you have heard him say "book" at night while selecting bedtime reading, point to each book on the shelf and slowly say, "Book . . . book . . . book. . . ." Then point to one book and pause as if you had forgotten the word. Hesitate just enough that the child pops out with the right word. There is a rhythm and timing to all of this. Point, begin to speak, and then hesitate with a pregnant pause. The child may speak up with the target word.

The goals are to allow the child to experience the process of saying words and to get him to do it frequently within the allotted time. The more times he spontaneously says words, the more familiar he will become with the process and the more voluntary control he will gain. For apraxic children at this stage, it is far less important to get them to say specific sounds or words than it is to get them to say any sound or word. The child will never know how hard he's working, because to him it will look like you're just talking and playing.

Design your dialogue and play so that the child has ample opportunity to say any word he pleases. Remember, the words are popping out at this point, and the child's role is to experience that.

Level 2—Dialogue

The child uses his pop-out words in dialogues created by others.

Once first words have begun to pop out, and once children begin to utter them more frequently, language-conscious parents typically begin to create dialogue around them. For example, after a child spontaneously says "momma," a parent might say, "Momma! That's right, momma." With a pause after this remark, the parent gives the turn back to the child and awaits his response. Thus, a dialogue frame is constructed with words just like it was months earlier with sounds.

Families present numerous opportunities for their children to repeat their spontaneous word within a dialogue frame. For example, a father might play a simple game in which he says to his child, "Where's momma?" while the mother is sitting nearby. Such a dialogue might sound like the following:

Mommy Dialogue

CHILD	FATHER
	Where' s momma?
[Looks to Mom and then back to Dad.]	Where' s momma?
[Looks to Mom and then back to Dad.]	Where' s momma?
[Looks to Mom and then back to Dad.]	Where' s momma?
[Looks to mom.] Momma.	That' s right, momma!
[Looks to Mom again.]	There' s momma!
[Silence.]	Where' s Momma?
[Looks to mom.] Momma.	There she is. There' s momma.

What is the purpose of this dialogue game? Obviously, the father is not concerned that the child knows where his mother is— the mother is right there and the child turns to her each time. Instead, the father is trying to get the child to say "momma" spontaneously many times in dialogue sequences.

Word Dialogues and Apraxic Children

Children with apraxia often do not have the opportunity to participate in dialogues that use their pop-out words, because adults don't create dialogues with them. There are many reasons that this can occur:

1. The word the child spoke may have been unintelligible to the listener. Thus, the listener could not make an appropriate response and create dialogue.
2. The child himself may not have waited for anyone to respond to him before saying more.
3. The child may not have seemed to be talking to anyone. Therefore, no one responded to him.
4. The adult who heard the word may have no idea that a dialogue could be created.
5. The adult may have broken one or more of the rules that govern dialogue.

Further Problems

Because of the severe unintelligibility of the apraxic child's early words, adults often make comments that squash the child's attempts. Consider the following dialogue between a severely apraxic child and his teacher:

CHILD	TEACHER
[Holds up cup and makes an unintelligible remark.]	What do you want?
[Again, holds up cup and makes unintelligible remark.]	What do you want?
[Unintelligible word.]	Do you want juice?
[Unintelligible word.]	Do you want juice? You have to tell me "juice."
[Unintelligible word.]	Say "juice. . . . Juice."
[Silence.]	J-J-J. Say, "juice."
[Continues to hold up cup.]	Do you want some juice?

This dialogue—which can seem almost cruel—is representative of the way many adults communicate with severely apraxic children who are beginning to say words. Their words are so unintelligible and so far from the mark that adults assume the child is not saying a word at all, or at least not saying the target word. In most cases, nothing could be farther from the truth.

Remember, the apraxic child has far better receptive language abilities than he has expressive ones. Therefore, when he is just beginning to say things that sound like words, he typically has been learning those words for many years. Just because he can't say them well doesn't mean he doesn't know what they are. Thus, the unintelligible gibberish that barely sounds like early words is, in fact, early words. These utterances must be responded to correctly so that the dialogue frame can be constructed.

How would a parent, teacher, or therapist perform better in such a situation? Consider the following:

CHILD	ADULT
[Holds up cup and makes unintelligible utterance.]	Juice?
[Unintelligible word.]	OK. Juice. [Gets juice and pours it.] Juice.
[Unintelligible word.]	Right. Juice.
[Drinks.]	

This much shorter dialogue is significantly more powerful and useful to the child than the first because the adult gives several clear and positive messages:

1. I heard you.
2. I understood you.

3. I value what you are saying.
4. I can act on your word.
5. This is how you say the word correctly. . . .
6. I like to dialogue with you.
7. I will be here if you say more.

Unlike the earlier dialogue, this one gives messages that build communication between child and adult and ultimately it fosters more dialogue.

What if your child is so unintelligible you do not understand anything he says? Apraxic children can be so unintelligible that when they finally attempt to say real words, we can be completely at a loss as to what they are saying. But unintelligibility occurs when we don't know what they are talking about. If a child approaches us with nothing in hand and no joint reference and he makes a remark, we may be at a total loss. But it's not too hard to understand a child who holds up a juice cup at snack time after having been served juice hundreds of times in this manner. To pretend not to get the message in order to motivate a child's pronunciation devalues the child's feeble attempt at pronouncing the word in the first place.

Therapy capitalizes on the fact that we can pretend to understand an apraxic child's words by setting up situations in which we are more likely to understand. The key is to listen to the child's every utterance and respond to each as if the child had said a real word that was understood by the adult. For example, I like to use small boxes of easily identifiable toys. I have three different sets of cartoon characters, one set each of toy dishes, toy food, toy cars and trucks, doll furniture, doll clothes, and so forth. As the child begins to play with the items in one of these boxes, I model how to select a toy and name it. Naming is my primary objective. As I name more and more toys, the child begins to name them as well. Now, no matter how poorly the child says the name, I know what the item is and can respond to his unintelligible utterance as if it were intelligible.

A dialogue at his level of treatment might sound like the following interaction with a Winnie the Pooh collection:

Child	Therapist
[Selects toy and says unintelligible word.]	You' re right. That' s Pooh Bear.
[Places toy on table.]	[Helps set toy upright.]
[Selects another toy and says unintelligible word.]	Tigger. You said, "Tigger." [Helps set toy upright.]
[Places toy on table.]	[Helps set toy upright.]
[Selects another toy and says unintelligible word.]	Piglet. I love Piglet!
[Places toy on table.]	[Helps set toy upright.]
[Selects another toy and says unintelligible word.]	Owl. See his book?
[Places toy on table.]	[Helps set toy upright.]
[Selects another toy and says unintelligible word.]	There' s Kanga. Where' s Roo?
[Points to Roo and says unintelligible word.]	There he is. Roo!

Apraxic children love this. I think that's because I become the only person in the child's life who consistently can understand him, word after word. They have no other situation in which someone can understand them to this extent, and their natural drive to communicate draws them to me. The child can name any item in the box, and I will respond to him in turn as if I knew what he was saying each time. With those words we begin to create a dialogue, and that dialogue sets him up for the next level of word imitation.

Level 3—Mutual Imitation

The child repeats his word multiple times within the dialogue frame.

After children begin to say words more frequently, and as the adults around them create dialogue, average toddlers begin to say their target word for a second and third time within a dialogue frame. This is a reflection of the stage Piaget called *mutual imitation*. Just like babies learn to repeat the same sound multiple times within a dialogue frame, so toddlers learn to repeat the same word multiple times within the dialogue frame. In the Mommy Dialogue above, the father works to encourage his child to say "mommy" several times in sequence. The child had difficulty back then, but by this stage, his ability will become strong and prolific. When this type of word repetition emerges in dialogue, communication between parents and children begins to be fun as key words are spoken back and forth like a game. A peek-a-boo dialogue might sound like this:

CHILD	FATHER
[Covered under blanket.]	Where' s my baby?
[Pulls off blanket.] Boo!	Boo! [Covers child again.] Where' s my baby?
[Pulls off blanket.] Boo!	Boo! [Covers child again.] Where' s my baby?
[Pulls off blanket.] Boo!	Boo! [Covers child again.] Where' s my baby?
[Pulls off blanket.] Boo!	

Once a child catches on to this verbal play, the bantering energizes him. Often the toddler will take identical back-and-forth turns until the adult becomes exhausted and says something like, "One more time. Daddy will do it one more time. Then I'm all done." Or the parent distracts the child with another activity.

That level of word repetition within dialogue is the cornerstone upon which the rest of word learning relies. The highly verbal and very articulate toddler will repeat words hundreds of times to master them. In addition to his word repetition in dialogue, the toddler will rehearse words dozens of times in sequence alone during solo play. Consider the monologue I recorded years ago as I videotaped a highly verbal 24-month-old child at play. Note the extensive use of word repetition throughout.

Monologue

My baby . . . my baby.
Baby . . . baby.
Baby baby baby.
Eat baby. . . . Eat.
Eat baby.
Baby eat.
Eat baby.
Baby. . . . My baby.
Eat.
My baby eat.

I videotaped this child talking to herself while playing alone for over an hour , and she talked her way through the entire session. Notice how many times she said "baby," "eat" and "my" in this short segment from her monologue. Repetition is a critical step in early expressive language development. It is the drill which exercises the child's ability to say specific words in specific ways at specific times.

Now consider the following dialogue in which a child who is at the one-word stage and his mother say the same word back-and-forth while watching a dog who has entered their yard.

CHILD	MOTHER
Doggie.	Hey, there' s a doggie.
Doggie.	Hi, doggie.
Doggie.	Why is that doggie here? Hey, doggie.
Doggie.	That' s a big doggie.
Doggie.	What' s that doggie doing?

The individual words spoken in dialogues such as this often take on a singsong quality. A parent who is a fantastic language stimulator will stay with the child and allow him to repeat and practice the key word many times before moving on to a new one. In the brief dialogue above, the child said "doggie" five times, and the mother offered the word back each time. This is another level of Piaget's mutual-imitation process: taking turns with the same word just as the adult and infant took turns saying the same sounds earlier.

Children love the opportunity to say the same thing over and over again. The famous Dr. Seuss capitalized on this phenomenon as a way to teach reading with *The Cat in the Hat, Green Eggs and Ham,* and *One Fish, Two Fish, Red Fish, Blue Fish,* to name a few. Dr. Seuss understood how to grab a child's attention through their natural affinity for repetition. But before reading ever emerges, children get caught up in this phenomenon at the pre-speech stage, at the early word and phrase stage, and at the stage in which a phrase like "poopey doopey" is so hilarious to a child that he falls over laughing. In fact, all the way through language acquisition, children's minds are drawn to repetition and rhymes, where they can learn how to make words the same and how to make them different. It teaches them to say sounds consistently and how to change the way a word is uttered.

Word Repetitions and Severe Childhood Apraxia

Word repetition in dialogue is a key to speech improvement, but the skills of this level of imitation development are missing in the severely apraxic child. As we have stated amply earlier, most of their words pop out, and these children don't engage in sequential word repetitions in either monologue or dialogue formats. They don't imitate themselves well, and they don't imitate others hardly at all.

A quick review of the sample dialogues in this book will reveal that apraxic children do not repeat key words in dialogue. This lack of word repetition leaves the apraxic child without an opportunity to learn sound and word similarities and differences, or produce them at will.

The apraxic child who is beginning to say words must be engaged in dialogue in which adults repeat his utterances in drill-play repetitions. Then the apraxic child will improve his articulation with word productions before he ever focuses on a consonant or vowel. This is accomplished by setting up situations in which it is likely that the child will speak certain words, by listening to the child's every utterance, by responding in turn, and by imitating the child. Over time, the child will begin to say the same word multiple times in sequence and improve his articulation. This skill will be used in all speech adjustments from here on, and barring other difficulties, to learn every consonant and vowel.

Level 4—Spontaneous Imitation of Old Repertoire

The child says his words in imitation of others.

After practicing key words in mutual imitation sequences like those described above, children learn to say their own words at the request of an adult. Thus, at this fourth level, a parent can get their child to say a key word without having to wait for the child to say the word first. The adult can take the lead, model the word, and expect the child to repeat it if the adult is modeling a word the child can say. The child now has it in his repertoire, and the parent can help the child apply the word to similar situations.

At this fourth level, parents can begin to show off their children's abilities by asking them to say specific words. For example, a parent might ask her child to say "bye-bye" as they leave Grandpa's house.

Apraxic Children

Apraxic children who are beginning to produce words usually do not repeat their own words on demand. Again, their words pop out and are made without much voluntary control. They need to learn how to rehearse the same word multiple times within a dialogue frame.

Once an apraxic child can repeat his own repertoire of words multiple times in sequence, he should be asked to say them frequently. If the child says "juice" many times at home, he can be asked to say it each time before he is given juice. The word in his repertoire is ready on demand. So, unlike earlier stages, he should be made to perform it now.

I design my treatment sessions in such a way that apraxic children at this level are put into situations in which they have to say the same word over and over to get what they want. For example, I have a track to race small cars. I give the child the track without any cars and ask, "Do you want a car?" When the child indicates that he does, I say, "Say, 'car'." When the child does it, I give him one. Each time he wants another car, I make him say "car." With 30 cars in my box, my goal is to get the child to say "car" thirty times within five or ten minutes as he plays with the toys. The racetrack works well because after the cars fly down the track, they usually fly off the table onto the floor. Before the child can retrieve it, I offer him another one and get him to say "car" again. I repeat this activity until all of the cars have landed on the floor. Then we put them away and get out another activity. Or we repeat it and say "car" another thirty times in a dialogue frame.

Although it is very important for these kids to repeat words, the drill is not drudgery. There is an emphasis on both drill and play. Between the times that the child says "car," he places the car on the track, races it, squeals with delight, looks at me with anticipation of the race, and so forth. We have fun while rehearsing the words.

Take the instance of Tom, who at three years of age had only one word: *train*. For several weeks we played with trains, trains, and more trains. We played with six different train puzzles. We drew train pictures. We loaded toy trains with blocks and small characters. We pretended to ride a train made out of a cardboard box. We even read train books. I got to the point where I couldn't think of anything but trains. During our sessions, and intermingled with all the other work we did, we played with and talked about trains. My goal was to get him to say "train" as many times as possible during an hour-long session.

At first, Tom could be made to say this key word only ten or fifteen times an hour. After several weeks, however, he was saying it fifty or more times an hour. That is a significant increase in the number of words per unit of time, a factor that can result in a greater expressive language experience, more fun with the word, and more desire to speak. Before treatment, the parents were concerned that Tom may have been too preoccupied with trains. They discouraged him from saying it because they were afraid he wouldn't learn any other words. Treatment was focused on the process of imitation, and they began to understand how they could take his obsession with trains and teach him to imitate with greater frequency and flexibility. Tom's imitation of "train" was followed shortly by imitations of other words he was interested in, namely "car," "truck," "bus," and "motorcycle." What a boy!

As time goes by, I may concentrate more on the drill and less on the play by using a game that fits colored wooden rings on colored wooden dowels. I hold up a ring, tell the child to say a particular word from his repertoire, and then give him the ring to place on the dowel after he says the word. Obviously, this is straightforward behavior modification. Not especially exciting, but fun for a while. I also use wooden puzzles by letting the child get a piece after he names it. And I use play food to feed puppets, ensuring the child names each item before the puppet takes the food and eats it in an amusing way.

An important part of my therapy at this level is picture cards. Using 3-x-5-inch cards, I draw pictures with bright markers and write one card per word based on what the child can say already. I do not include words or sounds I want him to learn; I make cards for words he already says. These cards help parents and other family members rehearse with him, and they can also be used for therapy. There are two goals: Get the child to repeat his own words multiple times throughout the week, and teach parents to listen to what the child is already saying.

Parents sometimes hesitate with this activity, thinking that they are not "teaching" him anything. "He can already say these words. Why should he practice them?"

I inform parents that the goal is to help the child say them at will. "You know how he can already say 'mom' when he wants to? Well, we want him to be able to say it anytime. We want him to be consistent about saying it and take control of that word."

Here's an example. Rama was four years old, hard of hearing, apraxic, and being raised in a bilingual home. At his first treatment, he spoke almost no sounds or words, but he did say "owie" and make certain sounds for the names of each of his family members. During the first months of treatment, I made numerous cards that depicted him and all his family members with "owies" on various parts of their bodies. With each card, Rama said either "owie" or his family member's name. This gave us about 20 cards with which to begin, a set big enough to have an impact on his speaking at home. Each evening, one of the family members would sit down with him and rehearse these words. Rama bloomed under these conditions. He finally had a way to begin communication and word rehearsal with his family. Shortly, I drew alphabet cards because they were of interest to him. By the time we stopped using these cards a year later, Rama had over 200. He was saying many words and short phrases clear enough for others to understand him without the cards.

Encouraging a child in this way is a form of freedom for the child. It allows him to speak more when he actually has very little to say. It also gives him a taste of the power of expressive language at a time when he has very few words with which to have power. The fun, freedom, and power that result from being asked to say words in his repertoire stimulate the child to speak out more words. As significant adults and other children encourage him to repeat these words over and over, he is invited into the communication routines of the household and classroom.

Level 5—Spontaneous Imitation of New Repertoire

The child imitates any new word.

After a child has mastered everything discussed in this book, he will be ready to imitate any new sound or word presented to him. Of course, the child will not speak the language right away. He will need years of speech and language development to learn how to say every consonant and vowel and thousands of words. Over the next several years, children put the finishing touches on their speech sound development. In general, they should use mature speech by the end of their seventh year.

Children with Apraxia

By now you know that an apraxic child's inability to say new sounds and words is the result of severe limits in imitation development. These children take a long time to go through this process, but most reach it in the end. Some—the most severe—do not. These children remain minimally verbal most of their lives.

A common workshop question is, "How do you know whether a certain apraxic child will become verbal?" You don't. Only time will tell. When a child with apparent childhood apraxia is a toddler or preschooler, you *never* can predict verbal success. To do so is foolishness. Some of these children become highly verbal by four, five, or six years of age. But because they almost all sound the same during these early years, it is impossible to determine who will succeed.

The stages of imitation are one of my primary tools for evaluating progress in these children. As the weeks, months, and years unfold, I carefully monitor how well they assimilate the skills of each stage. With this data, I can begin to plot their progress toward verbal speech in a step-by-step fashion. I can evaluate their progress continuously, even before they utter a single word. Thus, six or seven months into treatment, I can determine that although a certain child has not developed any words yet, he is on his way.

In general, if a child is gradually gaining skills in each developmental stage, I accept that he is making progress and will continue to be a good candidate for this type of therapy. However, if after six months of treatment, I see no gain in imitation skill at any level, I know that the child is not a good prospect for therapy at this time. More focus should be given to his augmentative communication system, and an imitation approach should wait until later. I usually reevaluate these children every three to six months to determine if they are ready. And I inform parents that if at any time their child begins to make more sounds, they should bring him in and get him started.

Sometimes there is a long wait. In one case, a nonverbal and mostly nonvocal child was monitored for many years. At the age of 14 she began to make significantly more sound. I saw her for a consultation then and again one year later, at which time the girl had begun to use short two-word sentences.

In another case, I saw the same type of boy when he was nine years old. In six months of treatment he made absolutely no progress. I recommended that therapy be discontinued. When I monitored him over one year later, he still had not gained any of these skills. In the meantime, he had added over three hundred words to his picture communication system and was using it in a variety of ways. The decision of whether or not to work on verbal speech with him was an easy one.

The following strategies will help develop your apraxic child's ability to imitate new sounds and words in this final stage of imitation development.

SNEAK IN NEW WORDS

Once you begin to see that your child can produce new words on demand, begin to sprinkle these into your dialogue. Try to rehearse one new word for every three old ones. His speech work will be 75% easy and 25% challenging, a ratio that encourages success. Adjust this percentage according to your child's ability. If you work on one new word for every nine old ones, your child will experience even more success!

SELECT NEW WORDS OF HIGH VALUE

When your child is ready to learn new words, select those of high interest to him. First words, like *doggie* or *cookie*, are more interesting to a child than words like *triangle* or *Friday*. Children with speech and language impairment may learn more difficult words earlier than more common ones. For example, one two-year-old girl with apraxia learned to say each letter of the alphabet before she ever said "hi" or "momma" or other early words. Know the interests of your child and select the best words to model.

WATCH FOR APPROPRIATE MOMENTS TO ELICIT NEW WORDS

Spontaneous imitation is most likely to occur when the idea of the word has captured your child's attention. For example, if your child is paying attention to the wheels on a truck, don't try to get him to say "truck." Instead, try to get him to say "wheel."

ASSIGN MEANING TO OLD SOUNDS

Help your child turn old sounds into meaningful words. For example, if your child can say "o" teach him to use it to say "go." Don't worry if your child cannot say words clearly at first. His articulation will improve as his imitative ability improves. Gradually begin to emphasize the correct pronunciation of new words.

FOCUS ON THE INTONATION OF NEW WORDS

Exaggerate the intonation pattern of new words and expect your child to imitate it. For example, say "Hi!" with dramatic intonation to make it stand out as something special. Be more concerned about the intonation your child imitates than the consonants and vowels he uses. Reward him for matching intonation.

FOCUS ON ONE-SYLLABLE WORDS

Children typically learn one-syllable words like *up*, *go*, *eat*, and *no* before they try to say longer words. As you model new words, select one syllable words over those that are longer.

FOCUS ON TWO-SYLLABLE WORDS WITH SIMILAR SYLLABLES

Children typically learn two-syllable words with nearly identical syllables before they are able to say more complex words. *Momma*, *dadda*, and *night-night* are simpler to say and more easy to learn.

FOCUS ON TWO-SYLLABLE WORDS WITH *Y* OR *IE* AT THE END

Children typically learn two-syllable words like *doggie*, *baby*, and *kitty* before they can say more complex words. Model these diminutive words over more complex ones.

FOCUS ON OTHER TWO-SYLLABLE WORDS

Children commonly learn other types of two-syllable words like *airplane, fire truck,* and *all gone* before they are able to say more complex words. But expect some articulation error. Focus on the child's ability to say the correct number of syllables over his ability to say the consonants and vowels correctly.

USE HAND CUES

Use hand cues on your face or on the child's face to cue word pronunciations. These hand signals help apraxic children grasp the number of syllables in the word and the sounds used to make them. Use signals that demonstrate what you want the child to learn. For example, shape the fingers into an *o* position over the lips as you exaggerate that vowel sound in order to get the child to round his lips more.

OVERPRONOUNCE MODEL WORDS

As you model words, say them clearly with a slight amount of overpronunciation. Its vowels and consonants can be heard, discriminated, and understood more easily by children, especially apraxic children.

MODEL WORDS SLOWLY

When you model new words slowly, your child will be able to hear the vowels, consonants, intonation, and stress patterns to imitate them more easily.

FOCUS ON CORRECT VOWELS IN WORDS

When modeling words, say the primary vowel with clarity. Then listen more for the vowel than the consonant as the child says it. Vowel clarity makes words more intelligible.

EMPHASIZE CONSONANTS THE CHILD ASSIMILATES EASILY

If your child demonstrates the ability to say words with one particular consonant sound, emphasize new words that also have that sound. For example, if your child can say "boo!", he may be able to say "boat," "bye," "big," or "bee."

DRILL-PLAY WITH NEW WORDS TO MAKE THEM AUTOMATIC

Devise dialogue routines in which your child plays with the same word over and over. For example, if your child can say "boo!" when a blanket is pulled off of his head, play peek-a-boo with a blanket for several minutes. Just like drilling on spelling words or math facts, the more you do it, the more automatic the responses.

BEGIN TO REQUEST WORDS

During this stage, children finally can be asked to say words on demand. Make lead-in statements, such as:

- "Can you say 'bye-bye'?"
- "Say 'doggie.'"
- "'Airplane.' You say it"
- "This is a . . ."
- "I see a . . ."
- "You can't say 'car,' can you?"
- "A cow says . . ."
- "The owl said . . ."
- "Where did he . . ."
- "She ate the whole . . ."

TEACH OTHERS TO ENCOURAGE THE CHILD TO SAY HIS NEW WORDS

It is not enough that your child can say words for you. He must also be able to say new words for other people and in other conditions. Show other people how to elicit new words from your child in daily living. This includes teachers, therapists, daycare providers, babysitters, relatives, neighbors, and any other person who has regular and consistent interactions with your child.

RECORD YOUR CHILD'S WORDS

Write down the words your child says, and add to the list as your child's vocabulary expands. Share copies of this list with others. It will be especially important to them if your child is hard to understand.

Glossary

alternative communication system. A means of communication used as a complete substitute for verbal speech.

apraxia. A nonlinguistic sensorimotor disorder of speech characterized by the incapacity to program the positioning of speech muscles for articulation, phonation, resonation, and respiration for the volitional production of phonemes.

augmentative communication system. A performance-based means of communication that assists verbal speech.

babbling. Sequences of consonants and vowels that infants begin to produce by six to seven months of age.

capacity to imitate. Aptitude, faculty, or skill in copying or duplicating.

circular reactions. An infant's chance behavior that leads to an advantageous or interesting result and that causes him immediately to reattempt, reinstate, or rediscover.

dialogue. Conversation between two or more persons that contains initiation, response, and ending turns. The conversation can be comprised of sounds, words, gestures, actions, and facial expressions.

dialogue frame. The back-and-forth conversational supporting structure for imitation development and conversation.

dysarthria. A neurological disorder of speech characterized by an inability to pronounce distinctly.

drill-play. Play designed to rehearse specific sounds or words.

first words. The first few words spoken by a young child.

imitation. The ability to follow in action or manner, to copy, to duplicate, to mimic, to reproduce, or to assume the appearance of a variety of movements, including speech movements.

initiation. An opening statement, or first turn, in dialogue.

internal image. The combined auditory, tactile, visual, and proprioceptive experience of a sound.

minimally verbal. Having few words.

minimally vocal. Having few sounds or vocalizations.

model. A sound or word presented for imitation.

monologue. Discourse by a single speaker.

motherese. The language of mothers to their babies.

motor planning. The ability to conceive, organize, and carry out actions, including those needed for the production of speech.

mutual gazing. The process of looking intently at one another for periods of time.

mutual imitation. The second stage of imitation development in which a child learns to repeat the same sound multiple times for their turn in a dialogue.

new repertoire. Sounds and sound combinations that children have never uttered before but that can be imitated after a model.

nonverbal. Without words.

nonvocal. Without sounds.

one-step dialogues. Dialogues in which each party takes only one turn.

pop-out words. Early first words that are spoken spontaneously but that cannot be imitated on demand.

pregnant pause. A pause in dialogue that functions to urge the next turn.

pre-speech. Before real speech emerges.

pre-speech vocalizations. Spontaneous, self-generated sounds made without correspondence to a specific idea or meaning. Used before real speech is spoken.

repertoire. An inventory of sounds or words.

response. An utterance made in reply.

sign. Hand and finger movements that have meaning.

spontaneous imitation. The repeating of a sound or word proceeding from internal impulses.

spontaneous imitation of old repertoire. The third stage of imitation development in which a child learns to imitate another person who models a sound or word that the child can already say.

spontaneous imitation of new repertoire. The forth stage of imitation development in which a child learns to repeat any new sound or word.

stages of imitation. The definable steps children take in mastering the art of imitation.

turn. A single utterance in a dialogue.

turn-taking. The back-and-forth process of dialogue.

verbal. Pertaining to words.

verbalization. A word.

vocal. Pertaining to the voice.

vocal play. The entertaining and amusing discovery of one's own voice and speech capabilities.

vocal contagion. The first stage of imitation development that encompasses the inherent tendency for speech to spread from person to person.

vocal synchrony. The simultaneous production of like voice.

vocalization. Infantile sounds made before words emerge.

willingness to imitate. Eagerness, inclination to, or predisposition to copy or duplicate.

How to Stop Thumbsucking $14.95
How to Stop Drooling $14.95
Pam Marshalla's How-to Series gives you easy-to-understand resources that help to reduce or eliminate your child's thumbsucking and excessive drooling. Includes practical guidelines, solutions, and activities for home or therapy.

Becoming Verbal with Childhood Apraxia $14.95
New Insights on Piaget for Today's Therapy
Particularly relevant for minimally verbal children who have been diagnosed with apraxia or dyspraxia of speech. Includes the organization and facilitation of early sound and word emergence.

Oral Motor Techniques in Articulation and Phonological Therapy $49.95
Includes all the basics of oral-motor therapy for improving jaw, lip, and tongue control, and for normalizing oral-tactile sensitivity. Written for both the professional and student speech-language pathologist, the text guides the reader through fundamental techniques used in treatment. An excellent supplimental text for courses on motor speech disorders, articulation, phonology, feeding, and dysphagia.

Order Today

1 Select titles

Title	Price	Quantity	Total
How to Stop Thumbsucking	$14.95		$
How to Stop Drooling	$14.95		$
Becoming Verbal with Developmental Apraxia	$14.95		$
Oral Motor Techniques	$49.95		$
Wholesale prices available on request			

2 Find total

Shipping and handling	$3.50
WA residents add 8.6% sales tax	$
Total	$

3 Mail order

Send check or money order to
Marshalla Speech and Language
11417 - 124th Ave NE #202
Kirkland, WA 98028

Questions?
(425) 828-4361
www.pammarshalla.com

Name:_____

Street:_____

City:_____

State:_____ Zip: _____

Phone: (_____)_____

E-mail:_____

MSL
Marshalla Speech and Language